THE
PERFECT STORM

My Journey from Heartbreak to Happiness

JESSIE RENEÉ

WESTBOW
P R E S S®
A DIVISION OF THOMAS NELSON
& ZONDERVAN

Scripture taken from the King James Version of the Bible.

Scripture taken from the Contemporary English Version © 1991, 1992, 1995 by American Bible Society. Used by Permission.

This book is a work of non-fiction. Unless otherwise noted, the author and the publisher make no explicit guarantees as to the accuracy of the information contained in this book and in some cases, names of people and places have been altered to protect their privacy.

WestBow Press books may be ordered through booksellers or by contacting:

WestBow Press
A Division of Thomas Nelson & Zondervan
1663 Liberty Drive
Bloomington, IN 47403
www.westbowpress.com
1 (866) 928-1240

ISBN: 978-1-9736-4012-7 (sc)
ISBN: 978-1-9736-4011-0 (hc)
ISBN: 978-1-9736-4013-4 (e)

Library of Congress Control Number: 2018911049

Print information available on the last page.

WestBow Press rev. date: 3/13/2019

IN THE BEGINNING...

"**D**RINK SOME STRONG BLEACH! I'M NOT HELPING YOU TAKE CARE OF NO BABY!" These were the first words spoken to me concerning my first unborn child coming from the father, my now ex-boyfriend. It was surreal, like I was on some sitcom and my ex-boyfriend had just made his very first cameo appearance as the stranger who was basically suggesting that I kill my unborn baby. Only this was no sitcom. This was my life.

Often people say that there is no testimony without a test. I didn't understand the meaning of this statement until I went through some trials in my own life. Not only are our testimonies the stories that give narrative to the ups and downs of our lives, but also our journey to overcome. They also give witness to the amazing grace of God. Testimonies are necessary to share because they give hope that overcoming adversity is possible. I have gone through difficult situations that made life and love seem hopeless. This is the story of how God set me back only to set me up.

I wasn't your typical high school girl. Throughout high school I didn't go to football games or the school dances. I attended senior prom with no date. I wasn't socially awkward, but I didn't socialize much. I had friends with whom I laughed and talked around the lunch table, but I knew there was just something different about me. I spent lots of time with my family. In my spare time I wrote short stories. I sang in the school chorus from seventh grade to my senior year. I was also a member of the school newspaper for a short time. I was a little artsy but not out-going enough to be a drama kid. The spotlight scared me, I liked to be in the background. We went to church on Sundays and spent time with Granny and the family afterwards. My weekends consisted of cleaning the house and grocery shopping with my Mama and Granny. My life was simple, and I loved it. I was never bullied or picked on. There was no question as to why I didn't do the things my peers did, and it was just me. Throughout high school I didn't have a boyfriend. I laughed and talked with the guys and I wasn't afraid of them at all, but they never saw me as a girlfriend. I had a few crushes, but nothing ever turned into a relationship. I always wondered what it was about me that didn't attract boys. I thought I was cute, was it my weight? I wasn't obese but I definitely was plump, but everyone always told me what a pretty girl I was. I didn't understand what the deal was. I didn't have any self-esteem issues because of this, I just knew it was something different. It wasn't until I went to college that guys showed interest. Even then I didn't know how to react because I hadn't experienced it before. Until I met him...

It was my twenty-first birthday, and some friends and I were out to dinner. These were the years prior to selfies, selfie sticks, and usies. Social media was just beginning to take off with MySpace and Facebook. We wanted a group picture and he was the person drafted to snap it. After taking the picture, he asked if he could buy me a drink for my birthday. This kind of attention was new to me, and I was flattered. I enjoyed my drink and when dinner was over my girls and I headed for the parking lot. Coincidently, his table was finishing up too. He followed us out to the car and asked for my number. A week later he called and asked me on a date. I wasn't sure because I was going home for the weekend to see my family. How was I going to tell my mama that I would be home a day later because I had a date? I was her road dog. Her partner in crime I couldn't stand her up for a boy. I declined telling him we could reschedule. I went to work after I got out of class and I saw a dozen roses on the counter of the copy center. I asked my co-worker who the lucky girl was. She was like, "Girl these are for you!" I was so shocked! Flowers? For me? Couldn't be. I read the card and it said, "I can't wait to see you tonight." I guess no wasn't an option for him, now I had to go. He had sent flowers to my job. He had stolen my heart. He was my birthday present.

I was excited to have a boyfriend. He was the thing I had been praying for. He took away loneliness and ushered in companionship and love. He was my first love, the first person I gave my heart to, and I was dedicated to him. I knew we were meant to be. I waited for so long. I was a sophomore in college and hadn't been in a relationship. This was my time to have the love set aside for me. Every time we saw each other I fell deeper for him. We hung out nearly every day. We both were from Georgia and had migrated to Louisiana, he for work and I for school. We were soulmates and I couldn't imagine my life without him.

He was my first love, my first everything. I got him gifts just because. I took my role serious in his life. He made me feel like I was the best thing that happened to him. I wanted to make sure I lived up to his expectations. I was super girlfriend. I supported him. The beginning years were going great. I was there for my man no matter what. Our relationship had grown, and we were discussing marriage. He wanted kids, and he wanted me to be the mother of his children. This was a sure thing and I felt like God had truly made my wait worth it.

When he lost his job in Louisiana, I helped find him another one. Every day I was on various job websites submitting applications. He received a call back from a grocery distribution warehouse. It made me happy to see that life was getting better for him. We went to the store and purchased a new shirt for his interview. The interview went well, and he seemed excited about his new job.

He lived with me while he got back on his feet. I paid the rent and utilities, we split the food costs. I acted as his wife. We played house for months, until he left the job, I found him. He moved back to his home-town. He quit his job at the distribution warehouse to work as a cook in a well-known restaurant. He demoted himself in order to move away from me. There was no comparison of the two jobs. Things changed. He was no longer with me all the time. He spent more and more time away from me. Distance had grown between us literally and figuratively. I didn't like it and it made me uneasy. I didn't want to be clingy, but I missed my best friend. I called him a lot. He missed my calls.

What happened to everything we built? Why was he falling back? He did a complete 360 and I couldn't figure out why. This was the beginning of my suspicions of his cheating. The change in him was obvious, even though he denied it.

THE SERIES OF
UNFORTUNATE EVENTS

M Y BOYFRIEND HAD GONE to Texas on a work trip. I called him, as I usually did, and he wouldn't answer. A short time after I called, he texted me to say good morning. Our morning conversations would always last the longest. He would ask what I had planned for the day and he would tell me his tasks he had to complete for the day. This day he didn't care if I had to work, or what I had planned. It seemed like he called to make sure I was breathing and that was it. The attention I used to get had dwindled to a brief check-in. As the day went on, he called and more short and choppy conversations. He was acting strange. Soon after, he stopped texting and wasn't answering all together. I felt neglected. This was about two years into the relationship, and he had already violated my trust. My private investigator skills were activated. We were on the same phone plan, so I began to go through his phone calls. I tried a few of the numbers with the longest call durations but didn't find anyone. I began to think harder. His ex, Tammie's number was on the bill a couple of times. I had gone through his phone and had her number memorized. Tammie and my boyfriend were in a serious relationship before he met me. They had been together about four years and split because of infidelity on her part. I knew he couldn't be with her. He had bad mouthed her continually. There was no way they were together. I decided to call her number just for kicks

I drafted my friend to call and we concocted a story. My friend would act as if she was from his job and needed to discuss an important matter with him. He worked offshore so getting a call from his main office while supposedly at work wasn't unusual. We called and my friend gave the ex the run down. She put on her most eloquent, professional voice. "Hi, ma'am my name is Nancy and I'm trying to get in touch with Mr. Donnie, is he there with you? After my friend's introduction Tammie said, "Ok ma'am, here he is. Hold on one minute, I will get him." My heart dropped, he wasn't at work at all. He was with his ex-girlfriend, Tammie. He came to the phone," Hello?" I was livid, "So you are at work huh?" "Who is this?" "This is Renée!" He instantly hung up the phone. My friend was so shocked she had urinated in her pants. I was in disbelief. He called me back later and gave me his story. He told me that he got word while in Texas that his grandmother had died. Tammie was the only person available to pick him up from the airport and that's why they were together. I felt horrible, so to make things right I called my boyfriend's dad to offer my condolences of his mother's death. His dad was unaware his mother was dead, because she wasn't.

My boyfriend had lied. We broke up. At this point it had been about three years into the relationship. The truth was coming out, the man who had once sent me flowers was beginning to look a little different. I was ready to let the love I thought was forever go. There was one problem, I had missed my period. I didn't keep track of my period, so it had been weeks before I realized it hadn't come. I took at test, it was positive. I took six tests, all positive. How was I going to tell him? We weren't on speaking terms. I called him over and over, he never answered. He was living it up with Tammie and had no idea he was going to be a father. I called his mother, I had only met her once or twice, we weren't close. I told her I was pregnant, she asked, and "Well what are you going to do?" I was taken aback. What was I supposed to do besides have the baby and take care of it? Was she suggesting abortion? I was twenty-three at the time, naïve, but abortion wasn't an option. He returned my call after I told his mom. He wasn't happy. He told me he didn't want to be a father. Abortion was my only option according to him. In the following weeks, he continued to push the issue. "Renée you need to decide when you are going before you get too far along. I can't have no baby right now!" He was infuriated with me because I refused. "DRINK SOME STRONG BLEACH, I'M NOT HELPING YOU TAKE CARE OF NO BABY!" I was destroyed. Who was this guy? I was scared and despite our split, I didn't expect him to feel so strongly about killing his seed.

A month passed by and he had cut off all communication with me. I was about four months pregnant. I was working one night and received a phone call. It was him. He wanted to talk. He came to my job, got the key to the apartment we once shared. He brought me roses, we went out to dinner, and it seemed like old times. I missed him. Even after all the drama, I was willing to hear him out. He got on his knees and apologized, he cried. He promised me he would be there from the baby and me. We reconciled and were ready to take on this new challenge in our lives. I had the baby. A beautiful baby girl. He was there with me the entire time. Life seemed to be looking up.

Months after having baby girl, her daddy had disconnected from the relationship again. He visited regularly, he loved his princess. When he left things became reminiscent of the past. I logged into his Facebook account and his last chat window was up. He was chatting with a girl name Tonya. He was low on money and needed help getting his medicine for his blood pressure. I had known and lived with him for years and was unaware of him having blood pressure issues. She told him that she would give him the money, but he had to have sex with her. I went to her Facebook page, her relationship status was married, and had two kids. Tonya liked every status my boyfriend posted and commented on nearly every picture. I didn't see her as a threat because she was married, and clearly, I was wrong. I confronted him about it, and he continued to lie. He said that she was just a good friend from high school. He claimed they were just classmates and the playful nature of the chat was how they interacted with each other. Every explanation he gave me didn't make any sense. He even went as far as having her text me to explain. I knew Tonya didn't want her husband to know, that's why she lied for him. She went along with what he said to save her own behind.

I was linked to this man forever and day by day I was learning he wasn't the person I thought he was. First Tammie and now Tonya? We fought about it. They had been seeing each other before I had the baby. This had been going on for months. This relationship had turned sour and I was over the drama he was bringing into my life. He tried to make it up to me, and he swore that these women meant nothing to him. He apologized over and over. He convinced me to bring the baby to visit his mom and family in his hometown. He had cheated twice, so I wasn't sure that would be a good idea. It was like going into the enemy's territory. He pushed until I gave in. His cousin was having a gathering and I rode with his mom. Where was he? He had been M.I.A. for hours and I was annoyed. Our relationship was unstable, and I was stuck with his mother and extended family. I wasn't comfortable with these people, I didn't know them. He finally showed up and called me into the living room. He was on one knee. A jewelry box in hand and my mouth dropped. He vowed to be the man of our family and promised me he was committed to me. Were we engaged? What was this? He took me in the back room and explained that this ring was a promise ring. He cried while holding baby girl and said, "I'm sorry for all I have put you through. I love you and I want you to know that I'm in it for the long haul." Then the truth came out. He was still conversing with the married woman. She was mad about the ring. I shared my happiness on Facebook, and she caught wind of it. She sent him message after message cursing him out.

He had painted me in such a way, that is was not plausible for him to commit to me. When she saw he had given me a ring, she knew then that everything he told her was untrue. He had manipulated the situation and I was stuck. I didn't know who to believe. I was sure that I wanted my child to have her daddy, so I turned a deaf ear to the outside noise. I'm wary of those who bad mouth other people but fail to mention their part in the situation. I had people hating me and I had no idea. He was bad mouthing me to anybody that would listen as if it made him look better. I was just his baby mama that trapped him. He didn't love me. He was just with me because of the baby. My character was being assassinated, and the man I loved was behind the trigger. I didn't believe him, but I was weak. I stayed.

There were many nights I went through his phone. My curiosity always got the best of me. Trust didn't exist in our relationship, and every time I went through his phone I found out about more girls. My boyfriend seemed to be everyone's boyfriend. The man I believed God had set aside just for me was community property and I had a difficult time accepting this fact. I flaunted our relationship and posted happy times, but all of those times were followed by heartache. His infidelity had gotten to the point to where a woman he was fooling around with called my job. Her name was Kasey. She was desperate for the truth because my boyfriend had told her we were split. Kasey was suspicious because what was depicted on my Facebook didn't match the stories, he told her.

The situation between he and I had become unbearable and I felt in danger because these women knew where I worked. Although these women were at least two hours away, in his hometown, distance couldn't keep them away if they wanted to hurt me. This happened on at least two occasions Kasey informed me that she was the sister to his mom's best friend. I could hardly believe what I was hearing. Surely his mother wasn't condoning the poor choices her son was making. Kasey assured me his mom knew they were dating because Kasey had attended my boyfriend's family reunion. Not only had she met his family she had met extended family. I wore the ring, I was his supposed fiancé. Somehow or another Kasey had gotten the pleasure of meeting family that not even baby girl had met. Her blood relatives that had never seen her face but had become acquainted with a fling.

I was puzzled how my boyfriend could carry out such acts of betrayal. I was consumed with keeping track of him. I never held him accountable. I had become so numb that I began to think this was normal. I had adapted the mentality that all men cheat. I believed that if I left him then I would be in a worse situation where he abused me. It was the lesser of two evils. I settled for less than I deserved. No one had ever told me about a woman's worth. I didn't know that I was worth more, I thought I was doing what I was supposed to do, and that was keeping my family together. I had accepted the notion that this was what men did and as long as he took care of home then it was ok. The craziness of us had warped my view of relationships and love but taught me valuable life lessons. The time I invested in running after him, I should have invested in myself. Don't waste time on people who have shown you they don't care about your feelings. Most of the time we try to help people be better because we see their potential. Never ignore what is for what could be. I was dealing with someone who had no boundaries with the lies he told, not even family was off limits. Yet I stayed because I saw the good in him even when it was overshadowed by the bad.

After forgiving him for those transgressions I thought there wasn't anything more he could do. I was wrong. The foolery continued. We traveled to his hometown to a SWAC classic football game. I was excited to hang out and have fun. One on one time with my love. We were enjoying the game with some of his friends and it was half-time. He went to the concession stand to get food and ended up staying a ridiculously long time. I didn't think anything of it because I figured there was as a hungry crowd. When he finally made it back, we ate and continued our good time. Well he took it up a notch and began to drink his dark liquor with no chaser. He was in a good mood and was doing it a little too big. By the end of the game he was sloppy drunk. We stumbled our way to his truck and his friend drove us home. When we finally made it to his mother's apartment, he had puked all over his game day outfit. The outfit I picked out and had ironed so nicely for him. He was a mess and I was really disgusted at how he was conducting himself on a weekend we were supposed to enjoy each other's company. I changed from being his guest to his care taker. We got him inside and he fell out on the couch. I changed his clothes and wiped his nasty mouth and cleaned him up as best I could for bed. His phone had fallen out of his pants pocket, and he had a new message. It said, "I'm glad I got to see you today." Who could have seen him today? I was with him the entire time, except when he went to the concession stand. I looked at the other messages and realized that he had met up with a woman at the concession stands and was texting her throughout the game. He was laying on the compliments thick, she was beautiful and everything else under the sun. Her name was Josie. Yet he was there beside me, smiling in my face while betraying me the whole time. I had put my hands in his vomit, wiped his face while smelling the stench of liquor and he had betrayed me. This was the same man whose balls I had rubbed Vaseline on after his first day on his new job. The job I had helped him find after he was fired from the last one. He had worked so hard and his skin was irritated, and he was in pain. I cared so much about his well-being that I was willing to rub Vaseline around his testicles to make him comfortable. That's how deep my love went. That's how much I cared about him, and he had betrayed me.

There was so much chaos in my life I couldn't make sense of it. I wanted to move forward. After one situation ended, we were forced into another. The hurt and betrayals kept building and I kept accepting them. I thought getting over his cheating made me a loyal woman. I didn't know hate was mounting in my heart. My heart was being poisoned with bitterness and I was oblivious.

He was dealing with older women at this point, I guess the younger ones were making too much noise. It really didn't matter the age, he had tried them all and no one was fine with being stepped on, no one but me. A lady named Kenzy called my mom's land line. Left her name and number and said that he told her we weren't together and that I was just his child's mother. She wanted to confirm his story, but I didn't have any confirmation for her. I only had the truth. Kenzy had recently had a baby about two months after I had baby girl. Was it his? She said it was a possibility. The little boy favored baby girl, but the paternity of the baby boy was never revealed to me. I had no words, there was so much recklessness going on that I had become lost in the shuffle. The shuffle of women, lies, and deceit. This was yet another one added to the list. It was getting longer by the day and the sad part he wasn't finished

It was time to move forward, so we were trying it again. It's so ironic that my only goal was to move forward, yet all we did was go backwards. By this point I had renovated my papa's house so that we could move in it as a family. The house had been gutted, new drywall, new flooring, painting, the works. Somehow, he was absent for most of that work. I'm not sure what female it was at the time, but I was putting in work. I was doing what it took for my family to live comfortably. I was also honoring my grandfather by keeping the place he had worked so hard for intact. He deserved that much.

We stayed with my mom while the house was being done. He had decided he wanted to work offshore so we were completing applications and were working on getting his TWIC card. It was Memorial Day weekend and we were enjoying family time before he left to start his new job. It was a celebration until I received a Facebook message from Quanda. She wanted to know why I was posting pictures and acting like we were a happy family. She was under the impression that he was just there to visit with baby girl before he went to work. I was acting like he was there for me and she knew that wasn't the case. She also explained his new tattoo to me. I noticed his new ink and inquired about it. The tattoo was Chinese symbols that he said meant family, but Quanda said it meant unbreakable. The tattoo symbolized the bond they had between each other. She believed they were unbreakable, and they had the tattoos to prove it. He was at my parent's house at the time waiting for me to get off work. I told her his location. She already knew it was just to see baby girl. She was confident in the information he had given her, because of the vow they had made to each other. I was the stupid one, how dare I put on a façade with a man that was hers. I was baffled by her confidence. On the other hand, I understood the power of his manipulation. She said she was talking to him at that very moment, and he had told her he was visiting baby girl. He had cooked for my entire family for the holiday weekend, we had gone to church. Was I delusional? I left work and confronted him. How could he be sitting in my parents' home talking to another woman? How could he get matching tattoos with her, but put a ring on my finger? He was disrespectful and I was tired of it. By this time, she had revealed he had taken her to a music concert and had made the pictures public for all to see. She needed to prove to me that he was her man. I believed her, but my issue was with the fool sitting in our living room, not her. I made it to my parents' house and asked him to step outside. We argued, he turned it up a notch and got louder. For the first time my parents were getting a glimpse of our troubled relationship. I made him leave and for the first time I didn't care about his well-being. It didn't matter to me where he slept, I just wanted him gone. Crazily this still wasn't the end. There was more to come.

Baby girl and I often fought for quality time with her dad. His time off was limited and he had figured out the perfect arrangement to see all his women and us, his family. It seemed as if the time went by really fast and we usually got three out of the seven days he was home. One particular time he was preparing to return to work, and he didn't call me when he made it to his boat. He always called, so I called him to make sure he made it in ok. He talked briefly with me and only texted afterwards. His behavior was reminiscent of the incident with Tammie earlier in our relationship. After I got off work, I called him like I always did. He didn't answer. I called him my entire ride home, the calls totaled around ninety by the time I pulled in the driveway. I was disappointed that this was happening again. After letting my guard down, he violated the minuscule amount of trust I had built for him. I went to his Facebook page and there was a new post. Friends from his beloved horse club had tagged him at a restaurant on the Gulf Coast. How as he on the coast and at work at the same time. I felt my blood pressure rising and I was getting more annoyed by the minute. After a little research I saw other member of the horse club with Facebook check-ins at this one particular hotel. It was the same we stayed in when we visited his grandparents on that also lived on the coast. My boyfriend was a creature of habit, so I called the hotel to see if he was there again. When the operator answered I asked for the room belonging to him and he transferred me with no hesitation. Once again, he had lied. I had begun to believe he was incapable of telling the truth at all. The phone rang a few times and a girl answered the phone. I immediately asked to speak to him and when he came to the phone, he hung up immediately after hearing my voice. I called back, "Reneé why do you keep calling this room?" He questioned me like I was the one out of line, like I had lied to him. "You told me you were at work; how did you end up on the coast with a girl answering your phone?" "Who is the girl who just answered the phone?" He had the audacity to tell me it was none of my business. I yelled more and cussed him more. I knew I was wasting my time. I just hung up and cried. I was emotionally spent. Sick and tired of trying and having no one to meet me half- way. Our relationship was a joke to him, but it meant everything to me.

I felt we were meant to be because it took so long for me to find love. I thought God wanted me to fix him, to help him be a better a man. I didn't want to wait that long to find love again, I didn't want to start over. There were some good times, so I focused on them and tried to forget the bad. I wanted baby girl to grow up with her daddy in the household. I didn't want her to visit him occasionally. I took his word and believed that we were teammates, but in reality, his actions were those of an opponent. His attitude was dependent on his relationships with other women. If he had a new fling or if things were going well with an existing one, he treated me like I was the love of his life. Sweet text messages and a million "I love you's" were all for me when his women were on their best behavior. At any given time, his mood would change when there was confusion in the land. He would be distant with me if one of his outside women were out of pocket.

I knew that this wasn't the place for me. I needed to find the nearest exit, yet instead I clung to him. I was so afraid to be alone again. Long talks didn't work, and my empty threats didn't work. I tried so hard. My reasons had changed from the need for him in our daughter's life to the fear of starting over. Although loneliness scared me, baby girl was my ultimate priority. She wasn't planned, but I thought that after she was here maybe she would serve as motivation for him to get his life in order. I figured that he would want to watch her grow up, to influence her, to help shape her character. He didn't care about any of that. Why did I think he would be a good influence? Did I really want a liar to shape my child's character? I had birthed a child with someone that didn't reflect the person I wanted my child to be. His morals were out on vacation. His limits didn't exist. The craziest part of it all, my influence wasn't what it was supposed to be either. I was accepting filth and I was ok with it. I didn't want my child to go through the situations I did. What kind of example was I setting from my daughter? I didn't want her to accept treatment like this from a man. I wanted her to never accept less that what she deserved. She had to know it was a must to demand better for your life and be strong enough to get rid negativity. How could I teach her these life lessons if I couldn't do it in my own life?

Even after expressing how much his actions hurt me, he didn't think enough of my feelings to change how he handled me. It was almost as if he didn't care. How could he not care? My boyfriend continually claimed he loved me. Was it possible to love and still ruin what you love? I wasn't sure he was capable of love. I had so many unanswered questions. I had no filter with him I was genuine, I put everything on the table and even with the outpouring of my inner most feelings toward our family it didn't seem to affect him in the least. How could I have allowed myself to get attached to someone who I couldn't even cling to? Love was within reach, yet it was so far away. I felt God was playing with me, why would he give me glimpses and not make it a reality? It was devastating to be right there and clueless how to make it happen, I became obsessed with trying to get my boyfriend to see I was the "one." I didn't know I was just digging myself further into a bottomless pit of hurt.

I stopped looking through his phone and Facebook account. My efforts were extensive to stop his cheating and unsuccessful. It was making me sick, it was driving me crazy. It hurt to love someone more than they love you. I was torturing myself, it was hard to understand why stayed. I felt that if he didn't want to be in a relationship with me, his easiest solution would have been to leave. I was making it convenient for him, he was doing what he wanted and had the benefits of a stable family. I cooked, cleaned, and cared for my family and it seemed none of that mattered to him. I begged for him to handle my heart with care and he continued to stomp on it. Was it really all his fault? I didn't take control and choose better for myself. My heart was hurting, and I didn't care enough for it to stop the pain. I was supposed to be ride or die. I was so busy being the wounded victim that I didn't see how I was enabling him. I allowed him to continually disrespect me and I never went to bat for myself. I accepted foolishness and then got upset when he didn't treat me better. I didn't trust him. He labeled me insecure. He promised me he loved me, and he swore that what he did in the past would never happen again. This was love? I was unsettled, sad, and felt unappreciated. I felt wounded and empty inside. I had tried my hardest, I had given my all. I had sacrificed my mind, body, and soul. Why did I give him control of me? I was so infatuated with the idea of us, that I fell in love with potential. I had given all of me to something intangible, an idea. I had invested all my time in a dang idea! We had everything we needed to be successful, everything except two willing participants. I was working hard for my family and all I got was disappointment. It was a crushing feeling. Even when I was at my lowest, I wasn't bold enough to leave. I wanted to pray, but I knew what God's answer would be. I had been given ways out over and over. I wanted a miracle. I wanted God to fix him. Our relationship didn't even feel right after a while, I wasn't even happy when things were going ok. The union that started out all smiles had turned into a burden. We had gone around and around in circles for almost nine years. I had suffered enough. The chances I had given had run out. I was at the end of my rope and I had suffered enough.

Ask for Guidance

"When you are confused, don't understand, and you don't know which way to go; look to God. Ask him for clarity, he will guide you."

ONE DAY THE WEIGHT was so heavy and my heart hurt so bad, it became unbearable. The strategies I carried out failed. I thought he needed more praise for his good deeds, so I reminded him daily of how I appreciated him. Maybe he needed more hugs from me, he pushed me away and called me clingy. I was all out of ideas and I needed to be free. I cried out the most heartfelt prayer I had ever prayed. It was pregnant with emotions, pain, it was full of a desperate need for change. I came to the realization that God was my only solution. It was time for me to be seated and let God step in to fight this battle for me. The bitterness and hate that had grown in my heart, I had to let it all go. I wanted feel anywhere near normal again. I told God that I was willing to do anything, even if it meant giving up the one person I had waited so long for. I made up in my mind that God's will for my life was what I wanted, but I knew this would be a difficult journey for me.

I stopped focusing on my problems, and redirected the issue upwards bring some form of peace into my life. Sounds cliché, right? "Baby just pray about it." Often, we pray and don't realize the work involved in God's solution to our problem. The guidance I was asking for required extensive work within my own soul, and I thought my boyfriend was the one with issues. I remember asking for guidance countless times before, and every time a new mess arose, and I never left. His guidance was taking me in a direction I didn't want to go, so I got off the bus. I wanted a magical solution that didn't require anything of me, I just wanted it to happen. God was showing me that my boyfriend's season in my life was over and I didn't want to accept that until I had no other choice. God had to break me down to the point of pure disgust for my situation. I reflected on our relationship's history and shame set in. I had no other choice but to give it to God, he was ready to flex his power after my muscle had been deflated. Some of my problems were brought on by circumstance and some I realized I was a factor in these problems. Many times, women go through things and we are part of the problem, even if we are not the offender, we are the enabler. Ask yourself: "What can I do to help improve my situation?" I knew what I needed to do but I feared losing what we had, I was scared to start over. I wasn't sure if love would come my way again, so I held on as long as I could. Until I realized I wasn't holding on to anything.

HE FORCED ME

"God's gives us a chance to move. When we don't, he forces us. He creates storms so bad, we have no other choice but to seek shelter from the rain."

M Y BOYFRIEND HAD COME home from offshore. We were watching a movie and he and baby girl had fallen asleep. I got up to shower and get ready for bed. I noticed a light in the guest room, it was his phone. He had gotten a text message. My first mind told me to not violate his privacy, but my curious mind wanted to know who this woman was texting my man. I picked it up, put it down, picked it up again, and swiped up. It opened! Where was his passcode? How was I granted all access to the answer to his faithfulness or lack thereof? I'm not sure what world I was living in, but I had really made up in my mind he was changing. Faithfulness was what I wanted, so I chose to be foolishly optimistic despite what his actions had shown. My eyes grew bigger by the text. Wider and more bucked by every picture I swiped across. Booty shots, nudes, private part pictures, promises and "I love you's." The words I thought that only we shared weren't special at all. This fool loved everybody. He wanted to marry everybody, he was engaged to not only me: he was going to spend his life with two women who were grandmothers. He was dealing with mothers of children that had children, yet he sacrificed his own child's future. He was so careless, the privilege to watch his baby girl grow up was being compromised because he wanted to be promiscuous. I was shocked. I had to wash away what I had seen. One had taken a pregnancy test, he was having unprotected sex with these women. Why did my life, health, and heart not matter? He seemed so loving, yet his phone showed me a person I didn't know. This wasn't the man that I fell in love with. After our troubled past he vowed to stay faithful. He made empty promises and became more clever in hiding his lies. My boyfriend was a scam artist, a man with a personality disorder, he was at least four different people. He changed who he was according to fit his surroundings. I wanted a father, family man, and future husband. He played his role, but what he didn't know was the act was over. I wanted someone who was the same in and out of my presence. There was a lot of faking going on and I wanted an end to this façade.

I gained my composure then went back into the living room. He was still asleep, looking so peaceful and innocent. I thought about beating him upside the head with a pot. I wanted to make him bleed. How could he sleep when he had so many devilish things he was involved in? His eyes popped open. "What's wrong?" he says. I replied "Nothing." I couldn't find any other answer, I had a million thoughts running through my mind. He says, "Renée I know you, now tell me what's wrong." I was calm and composed and I began to explain. "I went through your phone and I saw so many things that I just can't believe. You are carrying on at least four serious relationships, not including ours. I thought you were changing. You told me you wanted to be with us, why would you lie to me? You are not changing at all." He sat in silence, after all I said his reply was, you went through my phone? You went through my phone?" he was yelling by this time. He got up and went to the room where his phone was, I was right behind him. I wanted answers. He turned around and got in my face "YOU WENT THROUGH MY PHONE?" That was all he cared about, what I had saw, and what I had read. I had seen the truth with my own eyes, and he knew this was a wrap. The curtain was closing, and the show was over, so he wanted to make his encore performance one to remember. I pushed him out of my face. He charged at me and pushed me to the floor. I was shocked, we had argued before, but he had never been physical. He was backed in a corner and felt trapped, so he wasn't going down without a fight. He came to me on the floor wrapped his arms around my neck, he had me in a choke hold. What on earth was really going on? This boy had lost his mind for real. I begged him to just leave but he kept shoving me, I fought back, he was stronger than me. I was about to call the police. He took my phone. He didn't want the neighbors to know he was trying to hurt me. We had awoken baby girl. She was crying. She stood there in the middle of our mess listening to the two people she loved the most fight. He was still talking smack, but he didn't put his hands on me anymore. He told me "You are lucky my baby was here, because I was going to beat your ass."

Baby girl's family had fallen apart before her eyes. I didn't know who my boyfriend was at this moment. I looked at him in his eyes, but I didn't see the twinkle that was once there when he looked at me. I didn't see the man I had loved so deeply. He was enraged with anger. His eyes were filled with a fiery hate eyes, I had put fuel on his fire and the beast had been released. It hurt me to know that he could physically hurt me and emotionally. I was so broken, why did I look through that phone? What had I done? I had been battered, bruised and man handled. I had officially hit rock bottom. He gave me my phone, I had gone through his wallet, taken some money, and I figured if he was going to put his hands on me, he had to pay somehow. What was I doing? I had stolen. I had never taken anything in my life, no one had ever stolen from me either. I knew that night he had stolen the little bit of me I had left, Renée was gone until further notice. He finally gathered his things and left. Baby girl was hurt, her mother was hurt, and we cried ourselves to sleep. How was I going to fix this? I wanted to take it all back. I had no idea the change I was looking for would require this much, I didn't know that my soul would be ripped out my body.

THE DARK PLACE

"Life has dark moments, but it's in our darkest moments we learn our greatest life lessons."

THE NEXT MORNING I went to my mother's house. I crawled in my bed and cried until I fell asleep again. I was sore. I felt like I had been hit by an 18-wheeler. My lip was bruised, and I was scratched. I was at a loss for words. I was just out done. As the days went on, it got a little better. I told my co-worker about our big to do, she brought me flowers to cheer me up. They made me cry and sob uncontrollably. She just held me, I was a mess. I had sunken into a dark, gloomy place. God had shaken my comfort zone and I was distraught.

One of the hardest things to do is to lift yourself out of the dark place. It has a hold on you, it keeps you sad. It gives you the constant urge to cry, maybe even scream. This was where I resided. The dark place is where negative thoughts invade your mind, when the devil creeps in. Everyone has been in the dark place, the place where hope and love flee and give way to loneliness and discouragement. I felt like God had forgotten about me, I couldn't understand why God had left me, why he let this happen. I couldn't understand what I had done wrong, why things weren't working out for me even when I tried so hard. It's the crossroads between your past and future, do you go back to where you are comfortable, or do you take the leap of faith and go into the unknown? To get out of the dark place you have to be willing to be uncomfortable, unsure, and uncertain, all feelings that we hate but are all necessary on the road to your purpose.

I call it the dark place because it allows your situation to blind you. Some people get here and stay. It's so hard to see beyond what you're going through. Some dwell in the dark place, make a home out of it. It's important to always be open to hear a word from God in the dark place. Seek encouragement. I needed a word. I was broken after he left. I went to YouTube, in search of a message. I was able to find a word just for me. I heard the story of Simon Peter in Luke Chapter 22 Verse 31 when God told him Satan wants to have him and sift him as wheat. God told Peter that he prayed that his faith wouldn't fail and after he turned back to him his duty was to strengthen his brothers.

It was amazing to me that God allowed Satan into Peter's situation. God allows some situations to shake your world up just to reposition you. This was my light in the dark place. It was my answer to why I went through. God allowed it. I learned then that God takes us through things to prepare us for our blessings. He can't give us instant blessings that he hasn't prepared us for because we don't know how to handle them. It's like giving a motorcycle to a toddler. Yes, he has it to give, but does the child know how to handle the motorcycle? Just because we have it to give does not mean they should get it at that very moment. There is necessary preparation in the operation of motorcycles, a certain maturity needed to take on such an important task. A child is not ready to operate a motorcycle just as I was not ready for a serious relationship or marriage. I had to mature, study, take my test, and pass the test, to get the reward. In order to ensure we can handle our blessings as God intends, he must "school us." I knew I couldn't go back, and I knew I couldn't stay in the dark place. I had to trust God's plan and understand that his will is not to harm us. This obstacle was to strengthen me. It was time to put my big girl panties on and get it together.

On My High Horse

"Never build yourself so high up that God can't reach you. Always be available to him. It's a long way down when you're knocked off your high horse."

As I BEGAN TO reflect on my life I began to see the error in my ways. I realized I hadn't really acknowledged God before I was at rock bottom. I graduated in the top 25 of my class, honors cords, college graduate, job promotion, practiced purity, car, house. I was at the top of my game, but there was one problem, I didn't do any of it alone. I was so high and mighty that I forgot to give God his credit for keeping me along the way. Despite all the things that happened in my relationship, I remained loyal. My loyalty and dedication to our relationship gave me an even stronger sense of self-righteousness. I wasn't perfect and I knew it, but because my sins were different from others, I thought I was ok. I was wrong, just as wrong everyone else that I looked down upon. Was I any better because I wasn't sleeping around with different men? I still had sex outside of marriage. I was wrong. Was I better because I graduated twenty-four out of almost two hundred graduates? No, because we all graduated, my diploma said the same thing as number one hundred ninety- nine. In all things acknowledge God and all the things he has done. I'm not sure why I was trying to steal God's shine, but little did I know he would knock me off that high horse and put me in the position where I had no other choice but to turn to him. He had to show me he was God and put my cocky attitude in check. My excellence was because of his grace, and not by any doing of my own.

WILLINGNESS TO CHANGE

"Change can't be forced on anyone no matter how bad we think they need it. There has to be a want to be better in order for the process to begin. There's nothing more powerful than a made-up mind."

I FOUGHT THE URGE TO call my now ex-boyfriend, no matter how bad I wanted to. I reflected on the past years and all the emotions and hurt I had felt, I couldn't go back. Every day I reminded myself that the loneliness was only temporary. I had to stand alone, I had to be ok with Renée. I needed to spend time with her. I wanted to know how she felt. I wanted to know what she wanted to do in life. I needed to ask her if she was going to be ok. I had come to the realization that I didn't want to feel like I had felt anymore. Life had confused me and left me looking for direction. My comfort zone had turned into a hall a mirrors. Everywhere I turned all I could see was myself. My reflection, I had to look at me. Every blemish, every bump, and every dark spot I had. It was time to clear them up. How could I have imperfections? I wasn't the one cheating, I loved. I was looking for someone to hold me up, do for me what I couldn't do for myself. I wanted to be lifted and held up, but I didn't want to do it myself. I was amazed at how dependent I had become. God made me stand alone. He snatched the crutches from under me. He was going to make me hobble along with an occasional trip and fall. After some practice he knew I would be able to walk alone, to stand tall. I had to learn to do it on my own. I couldn't hand my life and self-worth over to someone else. They belonged to me and God was giving them back, giving me a second change to be Renée.

It was time to reel it in, get my emotions in check, and pick myself up. Baby girl was watching me, I couldn't just lay down and die. I had to find my inner most courage, and I had to do work.

As people we get stuck in our ways, we feel like we are fine. We are able to see the issues of others while ignoring our own. We all have an opportunity to grow. To be a great teacher, you can never stop learning. I thought it was all him and I was innocent. I was wrong too because I gave him the permission to treat me the way he did. After all I had allowed, it was really tough to allow myself to be happy. I wanted a "new thing," It sounds easier than it is. It's hard to evaluate yourself and pick apart everything you have done wrong or could do differently. The way we speak, think, understand and handle life situations are all key elements to change.

We always say "well, that's just the way I am." Where has "being the way you are" gotten you? Are you where you want to be? No? Maybe it's time to change. We learn habits from what we have been exposed to. I was a no nonsense, show respect, get respect kind of person. I responded according to what was put in front of me, treat me rude you get rude in return. When he yelled in our arguments, I yelled back. No one was the bigger person. I realized that when I responded with the same posture, I relinquished all control and allowed someone else to have control over my emotions. I looked at myself one day and realized I had to deal with opposition better. I had to get control of my responses to adverse situations. I learned to think before I speak, evaluate situation and decide whether it was worth my energy. Sometimes people say things to push buttons, those are the times when silence is best. Once you say your initial thoughts you can't take them back, think before you speak. Everything in my life was out of control including my mouth. Don't be the person always talking and responding. When you learn to be quiet, you will have more time to think, more time to observe. More time to take in information you may need to say something worth hearing. I realized then that this was bigger than me and I would need guidance from God to change the person I was.

You have to want your situation to change before you start the process. I had to get myself together so I could inspire others. My mission had gone beyond me, it was what God wanted. Stepping out of your comfort zone is necessary, I don't know why I expected change for so long and I was doing the same thing repeatedly. I repeatedly took him back with no consequences and then I wondered why he wouldn't change. Why would he change? He was doing what he wanted and was getting away with it. In order to get what you have never gotten, you have to do something you have never done. Being loyal is an honorable characteristic, but I was loyal to a fault. I had become a doormat. Even when I questioned why I stayed for so long, I had to accept that the situation was predestined, and it was up to me to use this situation as a push to destiny or a weight to my past.

You can't expect anyone to fix your situation for you. Faith without works is dead. I had to take control of my life because I was unraveling at the seams. Lies, mind games and constant disappointment had distorted my view of life. I was lost in search of my solution, but I didn't want it to be hard. Why did I have to make a move that I knew would make me sad? I just wanted to be happy with him, I wanted my little perfect family. I had become stuck, my personal life was a mess, my work life was a mess, and the odds were stacked against me. Until that day the lightbulb went off, I had settled. I had accepted things for what they were, and I wasn't willing to do the work to get my life on track. I left the dark place and entered the realm on enlightenment. I was ready to change, willing to do whatever it took to be free of the cross I was bearing. I had been tossed around like a rag doll, I knew I couldn't go back, then and only then, did the will to change my life show itself strong.

THE GENERATIONAL CURSE

"We model our lives after what we see. Sometimes we don't realize that we can make our own way, to be different enough to make a difference.

L OYALTY WAS INBRED IN me. I watched my mom support my dad, even when she was mad with him. I watched her cook, clean, and take care of our family. My mother had set the stage for how I would treat my mate. I had a great example of a strong woman. She also set the example of a woman who had settled. My mother loved our family. I watched her work and sacrifice for her family. I would hear my parents fight about bills and groceries. Sometimes it would get so bad we would leave and go to my Granny's house. My mom had learned from Granny. Granny was a dedicated wife. She worked hard and took care of five children. I have heard stories of my grandparents' relationship. It too, a rocky one. Papa was a ladies man: tall, dark skin, curly hair, a slim built man. My mom told me stories of how many different places she and her siblings lived. My grandparents were always on the outs. Even though they weren't perfect, I adored the men in my life. My daddy and my grandpa were hard workers and providers for their families. The women they loved needed more than provision. They wanted teammates, life partners. They wanted appreciation, foot rubs, and an occasional "I love you" I can't remember a time I have heard those words spoken between any of them. My maternal examples lacked and didn't demand more. I watched my mother make do. I had learned everything from the strong women in my life, both good and bad. It was a generational curse.

My Granny left Papa one day and never went back. They were still married, but they didn't stay together. He lived in the family home and Granny stayed with my aunt. My grandparents' estranged relationship had been this way before I was born. I had one aunt that was still married, and she was miles away.

Most of the women in my family were self-reliant. They made the decision to care for their families and not seek the help of a man. This independence could be looked at as honorable and was often celebrated. As a consequence, no one was held accountable for their contribution to the demise of the family. Where was the breakdown? There was a disconnect somewhere along the way and no one was doing the work to identify the solution. However, the family ended up generation after generation made the best of it. I didn't want to make the best of it. The generational curse had corrupted at least two generations of women in my family, and it seemed to be headed for the third and fourth if I didn't make a U-turn in my life. Baby girl and I would lack support, both financially and emotionally. I would have to make do and be yet another independent woman raising a child from a broken home. I had no doubt in my ability to care for my baby, but the fact of the matter is I didn't want to do it alone A change is necessary in my generation to change our future.

As a young woman that looked to the women before me, I saw strength. I also saw stubbornness and the unwillingness to submit and let the man lead. I witnessed strong opinions, self-righteousness, and double-standards. I felt like the men in my family needed appreciation and praise. They wanted to know that they work they did wasn't in vain and that they did get it right sometimes. There was no balance between praise and criticism.

Looking to the men in my life I saw hard work but not the softer side. The issues with my father were rooted from his mother dying when he was twelve years old. He didn't get the nurturing he needed. Whereas some men are nurtured too much and look for a replacement for their mother instead of a wife. My ex was spoiled by his mother and grandmother. It made it hard for him to lead our family because he was not used to making decisions for himself and could not be responsible to make decisions for baby girl and I. He had been enabled by the women in his life and needed a replacement mother and I was looking for a leader.

Over and over again these situations play out in our lives and we are left confused. We have to make the roles of the family clear again. We are raising children that are missing vital pieces of their upbringing because we have gotten lost along the way. God is the covering for the family, the man is the leader and source of protection followed by the nurturing mother and children. The generational curse must be broken.

I understand life's struggles won't avoid baby girl, she will have her own set of issues to deal with. I just want to ensure that whatever it is she faces; her foundation of family will support her throughout the process. I want that kind of example for my baby. Settling is not an option anymore.

Purpose in Your Pain

"There is no triumph without a trial, no testimony without a test, there would be no message if there weren't any mess, no finish line without the race. The greatest pain will reveal your destiny, endure it and it will all be worth it."

E VERY GREAT BLESSING WAS birthed out of great pain. I had to look at my own life. As low as I felt, on the outside everything looked great. I had a beautiful child, home, vehicle, and job. It seemed like I had life together. I've had people say to me, "I'm trying to get like you, you got your own house, car, and a decent paying job." It's important in life not to envy or want the blessings God has given others, there's a story behind it, a struggle tied to the blessing. I often want to respond to those and tell them, "I inherited this house after my grandfather's sudden death. He was found in that very house unconscious, and near death. So, you can have the blessing, but you have to deal with the pain that I experienced to get it. "Microwave" blessings don't exist. There's always a process.

When growth takes place in your life you begin to look at things from a different perspective. The pity party stops, and the enlightenment begins. You are coming out of the dark place. For me growth was understanding that there are seasonal people that come into your life to teach specific lessons and after their lesson is completed they go.

One of my greatest faults was looking to my ex to complete me instead of looking to God to be my everything. God would ultimately make me whole and there would be no need for me to find completion through anyone else. I kept trying to mend the brokenness by getting my ex to be faithful, but the problem wasn't him, it was me. I needed to let go of the relationship that was toxic. I needed to seek God to fix what was broken. I failed my lesson, and God kept administering the test. I was thinking so small that I couldn't see that this relationship I was struggling to fix was only a test for me. I was focused on the love I thought I felt. I was trying to keep my child's father in her life, not realizing he was permanent for her life, but temporary for mine. It's important that when people try to leave your life, you let them go. It's like Naomi, Ruth and Orpah in the bible. When Orpah's role in the story was over, she went back home. No one tried to keep her against her will, when she was done, she left. That's the same way we need feel about people in our lives.

I find it amazing that when I began writing my story, I believed that I played a part in the fall of my relationship, but I did not believe I had major character flaws. My ex's issues were on display. He was disrespectful, and often cheated but my issues were deep within. I had hidden issues. Insecurity had crept in. The need for validation from my ex dominated my life. The whole time I thought he needed he and God was shaking world up to correct the issues within me. God had a plan for me and the place I was in and issues I had could not function on the level he was preparing for me. The pain this relationship brought me was preparation for my blessing, testimony, and my purpose. The happenings of my life thus far took away the insecurity and gave me confidence. The confidence God would surely continue to take care of me if he had kept me safe thus far. I constantly needed to hear I love you from my ex, validation was necessary. If he didn't tell me I thought something was wrong. I no longer need that validation because I love myself enough that no one else has to tell me. Not only self-love but God thought I was worth dying for and that's all the validation I need. My life has given me experiences to pull from to help others and I'm grateful. I realized my purpose was to tell it and inspire someone else, and every time I talk about the change that came upon me, a new revelation comes. Not only did it bring me closer to my destiny, it made me want to know God more. I wanted to understand how he worked, what he stood for. The stories I heard at church were just stories to me, they didn't resonate with me. I never made them personal, because up until now I didn't have any experiences to perfect my praise. This situation helped me find my praise, helped me determine what God was to me. He was more than a man that died on the cross, he had risen. After they whipped him all night and drove nails through his hands and feet he asked for their forgiveness. They had hung him and killed him, yet he forgave them. That word was so strong in my soul because I couldn't imagine how he felt to have those he called friends betray him, and he found it in his heart to say, "forgive them." He knew he had to rise on the third day, no weight could be taken to the grave. He had a bigger purpose to fulfill. I realized that if he could get up from the tomb there was nothing that could hold me down, not even devastation. I had his "get up" power, he was my daddy, and I wanted to be just like my daddy. My need for more of Jesus grew, as resentment and hate decreased. I had to forgive, I had to go to the next level, and I couldn't go with this weight on me, it was time to free myself.

When it comes to problems in your life, praise God because it means you are closer to the things, he has prepared for you. It may seem hard, and you will get discouraged, but there is reassurance in the fact that from every struggle there are new blessings, revelations, clarity, and a renewed praise. Jesus could not have been crowned if it wasn't for the cross.

THE STRENGTH TO FORGIVE

"Let go of what hurt you, the longer you dwell on it the longer you are stuck there. Make peace with your past, look forward to the memories you have yet to make. Have the strength to forgive even when they don't deserve it. The condition of your heart is based upon the amount of weight you carry. Set yourself free, make your load light, and move forward."

I CAME OUT OF THE dark place, I was seeing the purpose in my pain and now I knew what I needed to do forgive. If I was going to go to the next level, I had to set myself free from the pain. Months later, the soreness left my body, my scratches faded, I had healed on the outside. It was time to heal my heart.

Many times, people say, "I forgive you," and we all know they don't really forgive you. Forgiveness is voluntarily process where someone who feels wronged lets go of feelings and emotions tied to hurtful events. It is necessary to release any urges to seek revenge, the urge to hurt or inflict the same pain you felt go away and you eventually want the best for those that wronged you. In their presence you have no tension, feelings of the pain you once felt don't remerge, and you are free of the burden you once carried. I've learned that when you hold grudges against people it doesn't affect the person, you're mad at, it affects you. It keeps you stuck in that situation, although you are no longer physically there, your emotions are. Your disdain stops the flow of your blessings. It keeping your mind clouded with thoughts of the past. It is crucial to your destiny to let it all go. Forgiveness is like a water hose. As long and it's tied in knots or twisted, nothing flows. Sometimes when you think you've gotten all the kinks out there is a slow drizzle. You have to go back look and at the hose again for any kinks you missed. Once you've gotten all the kinks out, that water flows full force. It pours just as blessings will flow in our lives once we have purified our heart. There's so much power in forgiveness. Unkink your hose and let the flow begin again.

Forgiveness takes strength. Many think that because you forgive, you are agreeing to the behavior of the accused. Forgiveness has nothing to do with what was done to you. One of the main reasons I forgave my ex was not because I agreed with his behavior, it was because of the mercy I would want bestowed upon me if I were to wrong someone. I realize that no one is without flaws. I could make the very same mistakes he did, and I would want forgiveness. There was no way I could hold anything against him and expect God to forgive all of my transgressions.

Another reason I forgave my ex was because he didn't make the mess alone. I responded to a lot of his actions the wrong way. I became a know it all, I had put myself on a throne and looked down on him. When driven by anger I spewed hate towards him, I reminded him every chance I got of how wrong he was, even though I was sure he already knew. I wouldn't let him get pass his mess ups. Yes, he was the one cheating, and yes, he told many lies, but it didn't excuse me from being spiteful. What part are you playing in your situation? Do you feel like because you aren't the offender, you have right to press the issue whenever the opportunity presents itself? It just makes you wrong too. Accept your role.

The last reason I forgave was because I wanted to be free. It had nothing to do with him, but it had everything to do with the condition of my heart. I didn't want to be bitter, I didn't want to be scarred, so I had to let it go. One day I texted him, I apologized for anything that I said to him that made him feel less than a man. I told him I wasn't mad. I also told him that I wanted him to be a good man for the woman that was meant for him. I wanted the best for him.

I can remember a time where I couldn't imagine him being with anyone else. I held on the fact that we were meant to be. When I told him, I wanted him to be a better man for the woman that was meant for him I knew I had healed. It occurred to me then that I was going to be ok. I wanted the best for him, and it was not fueled by my personal gain. It was only because I wanted him to be a better person for himself. The scripture was fulfilling itself, I was helping my brother. I was helping the one that once hurt me.

I was ok with extending the olive branch to him because we were parents. We needed to be on the same page. It wasn't about right or wrong for me anymore, it was about letting the dead situation finally die. It was about showing our daughter how her parents put differences aside and loved her no matter what their relationship status was.

I'm not going to lie or sugar coat forgiveness, it most definitely is a process. It takes the willingness to see your own faults in order to really forgive. It will uncover you, as you uncover what's in your heart. Forgiveness will have you crying never ending tears. The tears represent the impurities flowing from you, the hate and resentment flowing out. It allows love to come back in. Forgiveness opens your heart up to be filled with love and happiness again. It's your cleansing, it's your purification.

As I continue this journey to transform my life, I am reminded of the story of Naaman in The Bible. Naaman was a man of valor, highly esteemed gentleman, and a great solider that won the battle against Samaria. Naaman had a hidden issue. He had leprosy, a disease that caused swelling of the skin, as well as scabs. Leprosy was flesh eating bacteria that caused many to lose limbs. Naaman had a weakness that he dealt with behind closed doors. His healing was in the land of Samaria with Elisha the prophet. He had to go into the land where he had killed so many, the land he defeated, his healing was in the place he had devastated. Naaman was instructed to go immerse himself in the waters of the Jordan River seven times. He dipped repeatedly and the seventh time he was healed. It reminded me that if I dipped low, into the enemy's territory, in the muddy waters, I would be healed. I had one situation to handle, one more loose end to tie up. I tried to avoid it, but I had to humble myself, I had to apologize to my ex's mother. I assumed she was aware of the antics of her son, and I felt as a woman she would have let me know the utter and complete truth instead of choosing silence. I had to realize that I was not her child, her loyalty was to him. I had built up a disdain from her. I didn't hate her, but it was something in my spirit that kept me from totally embracing her. I also asked for her forgiveness, for the disrespect. I understand now that her only concern was my child, her granddaughter. I had to ask for forgiveness for my actions, I had to take responsibility for being curt, for not giving her the respect I should have as my child's grandmother. It was only right.

I felt completely free, my last bit of business had been squared away. Like Naaman I was healed, I had needed to go low one more time, dip myself back in those muddy waters in order to come out healed new, refreshed. It was done.

It's hard to humble yourself and let the whole truth be told. It's not easy, this thing called life, you must be willing to take wins and losses with the same amount of enthusiasm. When you lose, it's so crucial to not see yourself as a loser but to see room for improvement to take the opportunity to be better. One of the greatest things is to be able to say I'm sorry, forgive me.

FREEDOM

"Freedom is liberation. Burdens are gone, your mind is at peace. What do you need to let go of so you can be free?"

I WAS FREE. I DIDN'T have worry invading my thoughts. I thought about the happy times my ex, baby girl and I shared occasionally but my wounds reminded me battle I had been released from. I needed a change for my life, so even though I was having separation anxiety I had to stick it out. It was time to focus on Renée. I had to find me. I had to search myself and reset. I realized that outside of my little family I didn't have any interests. I needed them to need me, when that family structure was no longer there. It amazed me how I didn't know who I was outside of our time together. Baby girl was there, and we still had our time together, but things were drastically differently in her dad's absence.

My first step in getting back to me was getting control of my weight. We loved a good ole dinner date, so I had packed on the pounds over the years. I began an exercise regimen, changed my diet, and started to see results. I was beginning to love me again. I was under construction inside and out. I was taking control, doing the work, improving myself on my terms. I was proud of myself.

I was embracing my life without my ex, it wasn't as bad as I had thought it would be. I talked to God every day, thanked him for the strength I had found in him. I began to focus more on my relationship with God. He was the key to my future. I knew that with him every situation I would ever face would be easier. I was at peace. God had won this battle for me and had given me my mind back.

I put all the hurt and hate to bed and was ready to go head first into my purpose. Had God really given me this story to inspire other people? When I talked to people, they seemed shocked that my life had been so wrecked. I looked like I had it all together. God had sustained me so that the stress didn't show. Inside I was torn up, but God was healing me. I had gone from pure and utter heartbreak to happiness. He took my hurt and used it to empower me. It's so amazing how the things that once made me cry had transformed to be the fuel to my fire.

The love my ex and I had was tainted, I was now experiencing God's pure unconditional love. The love that died for me on the cross. I want to love like Jesus. The love that took on the weight of all my sins so that I might experience this freedom. I realized that the crucifixion of Christ had been a sort of fairy tale to me. Jesus' sacrifice was an event that came to mind regularly. Jesus had been nailed through his hands and feet to a wooden cross. He was beaten all night long. This wasn't a fairy tale, it was real. The blood he shed was real, Jesus had died for me. I owed him so much. He had given his entire life for me. I didn't deserve the mercy he had given me. No one else would have died for me. I wept, I realized that Jesus had done a marvelous thing and the least I could do was what he asked of me. It made my walk with him seem that much more important. I wasn't doing it because it was right, I chose to walk with him because I owed Jesus my life. I was his, he was my father, he never left me, and I wasn't going to leave him. He will go to battle for me if I trust him to handle my trials. I was strong enough to get up from the valley because my father did. He was my strength, it was all put into perspective for me now. I understood.

DIVINE PROTECTION

"Sometimes God's greatest blessings are not what he gives, but what he takes away. Trust God even when he says no."

I REALIZED EVERYTHING THAT MADE me cry, hurt me, and rocked me to the core, they all were God's divine protection. The times I cried the most, those situations saved my life. My partner that I entrusted my heart to was careless with it. Amid so much betrayal, I made dumb decisions for my life. I had managed to be pregnant twice since having baby girl. I want to share the story of the second miscarriage. Although both hurt equally, the second one hit me hard because I was sure it was God's second chance for us, and it was "meant" to be. Little did I know it was my greatest lesson of God's divine protection. Fast forward to my first OB-GYN appointment with this pregnancy. I had an ultrasound and was told everything looked good and was given the date for my second appointment. One day before my follow up, I wiped, and the tissue was red, my heart dropped. I instantly cried, this could not be happening again. I told myself it was just spotting and maybe it would be gone by morning. The next day the blood was still present, and it had gotten heavier. I called my OB and went in for an emergency appointment. My boyfriend was at work, so I called him to let him know what was going on. He sounded sad and told me to keep him updated. He didn't seem alarmed.

So, I'm sitting impatiently in the waiting room feeling my maxi pad fill up. I knew it was over. They finally called me back and I went straight to the ultrasound room so they could see what was going on. The ultra-sound tech said, "Hey Ms. RENÉE are you ready to get a good look at the baby? How far along are you?" I've never heard words so cheery and sweet make me feel so sad. I explained to her that I was having a miscarriage and I was here to confirm that there was no baby in the uterus. I assumed she hadn't read my chart. She gives me this look that told me she was very sorry and instructed me to get on the table. By this time, I'm out of my underwear and in the paper gown and as I get up, I can feel the heavy flow, flowing. I asked for a towel, but I was a little too late, the blood was dripping down my leg and onto the floor. I was beyond embarrassed and there was nothing I could do, in this moment, to fix it. This was happening to me again and this time I was bleeding all over the place. I was alone. I lost it. The tears began to flow, and I felt so helpless. The ultrasound tech tried to console me, and she assured me it was ok that she would clean it up.

After my breakdown I got on the table, she did the exam, and gave me the news of the inevitable. By this point I was numb, I just wanted it to be over so I could go home. The ultrasound tech apologized again and instructed me to get dressed so I could talk to the doctor about my scan.

This seemed to be the longest appointment of my life. After it was all over, I called him, I told him I had lost the baby. He asked, "Well, did they tell you why this keeps happening?" I told that him the doctor said there is really no explanation for it, it's just something that happens in pregnancy and that if it happened a third time then they would do further testing. He pitched a fit, "Reneé that's bull crap, how do you keep having miscarriages and they can't tell you why? That's stupid!" I was speechless, it wasn't what I needed to hear, I wanted to be consoled, I wanted a hug, I needed to hear "Baby, I'm coming home as soon as possible, it will be ok we will try again." I knew that wasn't the kind of man I was dealing with, I knew he would take the situation and make it about what someone was doing wrong. I wanted answers too, but I also wanted support and compassion. I was alone and he was drilling me for answers I didn't have. ALONE! I just wanted it to be over. After going through miscarriages, I had looked pass the hurt, only to realize there I wasn't ready to a mom again. It wasn't in his plan for me to be a mother of the babies I lost. It's a story I don't tell, and few know. I had hidden pains that no one know about. I had cried tears that none except a mother who had gone through miscarriage would understand. Going through it was tough, but there is so much consolation in the fact that God will restore everything I lost if I just follow him. As I write this tears flow, it still hurts. I know many times our blessings are not what he gives us but what he takes away. I didn't realize that my heart had endured so much until I began telling my story.

CONFLICTING PLANS

"Sometimes our plan must fall apart, for God's plan to come together. Trust him, even when it hurts."

EVERYONE HAS AN IDEA of how they want their life to play out. The job, ideal mate, car, whether to have kids, their version of the American Dream. We have visions of the big beautiful house, the pretty green grass, everything is perfect in our plan. Trials are nonexistent and the good guys always win. In our plan fairness and doing what's right is the way of the world according to what we want for our lives.

So, what happens when our plan and God's divine plan conflict? What we planned for ourselves is not fulfilling itself. We had not prepared ourselves for hardships, disappointment, and for mistakes. When we see things are going left, we always say, "Nothing is turning out right for me." But "right" according to who? Sometimes when things go wrong according to our plan, it's right on track with God's plan. We have a misunderstanding when it comes to our steps being ordered by the Lord. We assume that all the good steps are ordered by him and the bad ones are our fault or the devil. The funny thing is, he orders the wrong ones too. Many times, before great triumph, there is a great trial. Things must fall apart before they can come together.

It hurts so badly though. It's hard to understand why God would put us through these tough times, I asked plenty of times "Lord, what did I do that was so bad that you have to take me through this?" Everything is falling apart for you and coming together for someone else. It will make you question yourself. Did I pray enough? Did I cuss too much? Maybe I didn't put in enough time at church? Life will make you question yourself but be certain of one thing: God wants everything to be well with us. That statement does not mean everything will come easy or without adversity, it means that after the hard times, after you've cried, realize that all things work for your good. I cried many nights over my situation. Now looking back, I see that without those tears I wouldn't have anything to say, I would have no testimony. I don't think I would have the same drive because I would have no motivating force behind me.

Sometimes we pray and our prayers aren't answered. What do you do when you sent up your most sincere prayer and God is silent? How do you handle disappointment when you were certain that God heard your cry? The answer is simple but remains one of the hardest things to do: Trust God.

How can I trust him when my world is falling apart, I have no way to recover, and it seems all hope is lost? The hurt you feel is rooted deep in your soul, and you have no other option but to give up. I questioned God "Lord I prayed so hard, and Lord you knew I needed this blessing, why didn't you give it to me?" It's so hard to understand why the thing you thought was meant for you doesn't work out. God knows what we need, and when he denies us what we really want, we have to understand that it was not for us. I cried many nights because I had a hard time dealing with the fact that my boyfriend didn't love me the same way I loved him. The best solution was to end our relationship but because I wasn't ready to accept that realization I held on too long.

One of the biggest mistakes is that we view God as a life line after we've gotten in sticky situations. He's often the last resort. We treat God as if he is here to serve us and help us carry out our plans we have for our lives. God created each of us for a specific purpose. We are here to help him fulfill his divine plan. God has given everyone talents, or some unique characteristic that serves as a clue to our purpose. All we have to do is ask him what he wants us to do.

Often, we go from profession to profession searching for the thing that fulfills us and repeatedly end up empty. It's because we haven't asked God his will for our lives. When we consult with God the path we take, then he will provide the resources we need to make it happen. God wants to be our first resort and not the last.

Looking back I see that I had no trust in God, my primary focus was my desires. I didn't ask God what he wanted for me, that's why my world was turned upside down. God had to bring me to my lowest only so I would look up. It's so comforting to know that God didn't hate me. After two miscarriages and countless heartbreaks I seriously thought he had beef with me. I later realized he was making me stronger, getting me ready for his plan. He knew what I needed to be properly equipped for my journey. I have accepted the place I'm in and I have where I came from. Without those places I wouldn't be prepared to go where he's taking me. The bigger the pain, the bigger the blessing.

I was attached to the idea of how great my family could be. I wanted us to get pass all the drama and lies, but we never did. I realized Renee's plan had failed miserably, it was time to let go and put my plan to bed. God's divine plan was now activated, I was ready. The road to destiny is full of detours but they always lead you back to your destined path.

Distractions

"Nothing should take you from the will of God. If it changes you for the worse, you need to let it go."

M Y RELATIONSHIP WAS A big distraction from everything that needed my attention. I had become consumed with making sure he was faithful. I had made it my life's mission to keep him on track, to ensure his loyalty, and transform him into a good and honest man. I was focused on fixing his character and in the process damaged mine. Anger that I couldn't contain grew inside of me when he didn't answer the phone and when he didn't call me back. I had given him complete control of my emotions. My days, good or bad, depended on his actions. Why didn't I have control of my happiness? Happiness is a choice, and I had allowed someone else to choose for me. I wanted him to care about the condition of my heart that I had placed in his hands. I waited from my boyfriend to realize the vital role I had given him in my life as my heart's keeper. I accepted entirely too much foolishness waiting on that miracle, the miracle that I wanted for us, but he didn't. We didn't have the same goals, we were in different places, unequally yoked. I had broken myself trying to fix someone else. My heart was so involved, that my attitude changed, my spirit had left me. My charisma was gone, my smile wasn't backed by happiness, and when glimpses of joy appeared, they didn't stay long. I had gotten to such a low place that I felt numb. When we had good times, I still had a feeling of sadness as much as I enjoyed myself, I knew it wouldn't last long. I knew drama was on the horizon. I couldn't even be happy with happiness. The dinner dates, road trips, and play dates all made us smile. Why couldn't that be enough? I never understood why it wasn't enough for him to be with us. These were times that baby girl and I adored, moments we didn't want to end, but it seemed that his mind was somewhere else, somewhere away from his physical location. The things that gave us great joy didn't stimulate him at all. He was distracted. What is distracting you from your destiny? It's so important to do some house cleaning. Distractions can be people, habits, as well as the way we think. Many times, we get caught up in things that do not take us closer to our destiny. They take up time and space and have no real value to the bigger picture we are trying to paint. My boyfriend was a lover of horses and it took of a lot of his time. Often the horses came before baby girl and me. To his family, the horses seemed to be a distraction because they kept him away from what should have been more important. When God has given you clear direction on your purpose, distractions will arise but become more difficult at being successful because of your focus. Daily I remind myself of the promise God made me and take steps to achieve it. Distractions come to deter us from receiving God's promise, but it takes daily effort to stay on track and get what has for us. The relationship I have developed with God has to be nurtured every day. I wake up and pray. I pray in the middle of the day. When I think of how he woke me up I say thank you. To fight off distractions you have to be continually connected to the Father.

After the Storm

"After every storm the sun shines again"

AFTER IT'S ALL SAID and done, who are you outside of your trials? What lessons have you taken away from residing in dark places? When everything is settled, who are you? What's the thing that you love to do? What are you passionate about? These were questions that I previously didn't have the answer to. My situation was the only thing that defined me, the only thing I cared about. When I began dating again, some of the first questions I was asked were, "What do you like to do?" and "Tell me about yourself." After coming up blank, I realized I really didn't know. My life, for eight years, had revolved around my little family. Everything I stood for was defined by those two, how could I not know myself? I had to find myself, I had to get back to me.

Before I started my journey find myself, I had to make sure baby girl was in a good space. She was my top priority. I couldn't be there with her all the time because my job kept me away, but I knew she needed me, because I needed her. She gave a million hugs in a day and the way I was feeling, I needed them. I wanted the best for my baby, and it hurt me so bad to be away from her. I didn't want her to feel abandoned by her parents because we both worked. The difference was that I came but he stopped trying to see her. I felt like he left me alone to deal with the aftermath. I knew we weren't going to work, but it puzzled me as to why I had to answer the tough questions baby girl asked. I felt cheated because I wasn't the one that violated our commitment, he was. I wanted him to answer for himself. Part of being a single mother is having to deal with difficult situations like this. I understood the position I placed myself in, so I didn't ignore the damage that could possibly be done to my baby. I wanted to prevent it. Baby girl was not only confused, but she was also super emotional. It was her first year at big girl school, kindergarten, and she was excited. The reality of her daddy not being there brought her to tears. He called to see how her day went but it didn't seem to console her. She cried for the first two weeks. She couldn't understand why he didn't pick her up from school like he used to. I wanted to make it better, but she wanted her daddy back. I couldn't be her dad, it was out of my control. I felt guilty because he wasn't coming back, he didn't make any effort to shield her from the result of our failed relationship. He continued with his life and never missed a beat. I was fine with him getting her from school and them hanging out, he never asked though. I didn't want to be in a toxic situation just because we had a child, I wanted it to be because of love. He would call but for some reason he prolonged his face to face meeting with baby girl after our split. Beyond the betrayals and harsh words, we had one thing that linked us for life, and baby girl was it. Occasionally, she would ask when he was coming to see her. I didn't have a concrete answer because I wasn't sure, I would just tell her soon. I hated not knowing, she was looking to me for an answer that I couldn't give her. It had been about 4 months, and we visited a church that was in his home town. When baby girl got wind of our location, she asked to see her grandma. My first mind told me to say no, but I knew that would be selfish. So, despite of how I felt, I took her. She had other family and I couldn't let my own reasons stop her from spending time with her family. She wasn't just mine, her blood was a mix of both of us.

To grandmother's house we went, I put on a smile and granted her wish. I was confused as to why she didn't ask for her daddy. Maybe she didn't want the rejection. He was in town, and he also came over to visit. It was the first time he had laid eyes on her in four months and you could tell they missed each other. The moment was bittersweet. I was glad she got to see him, but I knew the moment wasn't going to last because we had to go back home. He promised her he would see her later in the week, and he kept his promise. She was doing much better and I was happy. He was happy. I knew it was a tough situation for all of us, so I was patient. I knew we were living our life out of order, having children before marriage. These are the issues we must deal with. I am grateful that God is willing to give us all another chance, his grace has kept me even when I didn't deserve it. I was willing to make it right with God, willing to live my life right the second time around.

I prayed for my baby because no matter how tumultuous our relationship was, she needed her daddy. I didn't want her to have any resentment, so I made sure she only heard positive things from me when it came to him. He was a good dad to her, and I understood that the situation was tough and maybe he didn't know how to go about it all. Ignoring her was not the way to handle the situation. I had to talk with him, express my concern and make it known that he needed to keep in contact with her.

Now it was time to keep doing the work on myself. I searched myself and immersed myself in the word of God. I listened to at least two sermons throughout the course of a day and read on my bible app. I needed encouragement stored up so whenever there was an attack, I would be ready and filled with ammunition to battle to the end. Once I understood that God was with me through it all, my relationship with him grew. I began to seek out my purpose in life, what I was put here to do. My life thus far had to have had a purpose outside of the hurt. What was my next step? Dating, a hobby, a new job? I was a mother first, but I didn't want that to be all that I was.

I decided to put myself first. It was time to live in my purpose and fulfill what God had created me to do. He showed me that after the storm, I had to tell it. Talk about the hurt, the pain, the loneliness, the heartbreak, and the rain. I attempted to battle the storm alone instead of finding shelter in God. I didn't understand how I would tell it, though. I didn't even understand why I had to, because heartbreaks and bad relationships are a dime a dozen. But so many women are scarred by what they experience in relationships to the point, they don't even realize what it has done to them. My mama said, "Girl you could write a book, you've been through so much." So, my lightbulb went off, I used to write short stories when I was younger. Then doubt set in, how in the world was I going to write an entire book? How was I going to get it published? I was broke, single, and had bills to pay. A book was nowhere in my budget. Was this the gift that was buried inside of me? Was my relationship the push of something that I needed to birth? Who would be my audience, would my gifts really make room for me? I had so many questions, but I had to exercise my faith and take that leap. I started, I stopped, and I started and stopped again. I would post whatever was on my heart on Facebook, my aunt commented and said "Renée, where is all this wisdom coming from? I see a book in the works, you have something your generation needs to hear." That was confirmation. It was the word I needed to tell me I was on the right path. God will send a messenger in the person you least expect. This was my great aunt, miles and miles away, totally removed from my situation. She knew nothing of what I'd faced, but she sensed my passion.

So, when I began writing this book, I realized it was therapeutic. I realized that I had grown more than I realized. I thought I would never be able to live without him, but I was stronger than I had given myself credit for. There are many young ladies that lack happiness because of being misused because it is almost impossible to repair your heart when you don't know how. It's not easy to move your mountains when you can only focus on the mountain. Start thinking of strategies to climb that mountain. How are you going to get to the other side? Be willing to do whatever it takes, and never look back on what you left behind, because what's on the other side is all that matters. If you are committed to the promise that God has for you, it will not return void. He cannot lie, he will fulfill his promises, but it requires your total commitment.

Life became so much better when I realized the strength God had given me. I realized how wonderful it was not to carry such weight. I was working on a complete over haul. I had to renew myself. I had become stuck, but little by little I was coming out. You can too. It takes strength, resilience, tenacity, faith, and commitment. Don't give up, your pain serves a purpose. Don't stop until you find discover it. Your destiny is greater than anything that you have been through. People will call you crazy and they won't understand, but they don't know what you are chasing after. All you need is the vision and God's promise. I have learned that the validation from people is irrelevant, God validation is the only confirmation you need. It will get hard, and you may want to give up, but always remember that God's keeps his promises. Every day must start on a positive note. Every day I open my eyes I give thanks for another day, throughout my day when I think of the goodness of what God has done for me, I say thank you. When adverse situations challenge me, I give thanks. When you keep God at the center of your being, he has the power to safely guide your steps throughout the day.

WE CAN DEPEND ON DADDY

"The most dependable man I know, died for me, he freed me from sin, and he knew me before I knew myself. Even when I put my trust in man, he forgave me. My heavenly father has never let me down."

IT WAS BABY GIRL's birthday. She was growing right before my eyes. I couldn't believe she was turning six years old! It was years ago I fought to keep my baby. I fought to keep the child her daddy didn't want live. The child her grandmother questioned, "Well what you going to do?" I let her live, that's what I did. I had given life to a beautiful curly headed sophisticated little princess and I loved her to the moon and back. I was so proud to be her mama. It was her birthday and we were going to celebrate her life. All her birthday parties were an event to attend and I always went above, because I almost didn't have her. She almost didn't make it. The balloons were up, the cake was in place. Her daddy was bringing the pizza and paying for venue. He called and told me he was running late, so he needed me to go get the pizza. It wasn't what I had planned but I went anyway. No fuss, I just went. I came back with the pizza, where was baby girl? She came running through the venue, "Mama! I love this place, it's so fun! Can we have my birthday party every year?" She was enjoying her party and I was happy. Her daddy called again. He was upset. "I'M NOT COMING TO THE PARTY!" "Wait, what?" "I'M NOT COMING BECAUSE SOMEONE BROKE IN MY TRUCK. THEY STOLE MY GUN AND HER GIFTS IN THE BACKSEAT!" "So why aren't you still coming to the party?" "I HAVE TO GO MAKE A POLICE REPORT ASAP RENÈE, IT CANNOT WAIT!" "I don't understand why you can't do that tomorrow. If something happens with the gun, you have thirty plus people to account for your whereabouts. Baby girl is going to be upset, she was looking forward to seeing you. You were supposed to pay for the party place, what am I supposed to do?" "RENÈE, I CAN'T COME. YOU DON'T HAVE ANYONE THERE THAT CAN GIVE YOU THE MONEY FOR THE PLACE?" By this point I was livid, I was aggravated to the max, and I realized why I had left our relationship. He wasn't dependable. After all the hard times in our relationship, I managed to still let my guard down. I knew he wasn't dependable when it came to matters concerning me, but baby girl's birthday was always a sure thing. Was he embarrassed because he had been absent since our breakup? It had been about four months and he hadn't been around my family since then. Or did someone really steal her gifts? I asked the venue if they would take a debit card over the phone. They agreed. He gave me the number. "Ma'am, can you give me the number again it's not approving the card?" I called him again verify the card number and billing address and the card still declined. I was upset! It didn't concern him that his card was being declined. I had purchased decorations, additional food to compliment the pizza, party favors, her birthday outfit, and the deposit on the venue, I was spent out. I was depending on him to fulfill his end of our deal and pay the last expenses. He had let me down and hung up the phone in my face. I wasn't planning on spending an additional $125, but I had to pay for the venue or get out. I paid the remaining balance, with no hope of getting paid back. Baby girl was still playing. She had no idea that her daddy wasn't coming. I knew I would have more questions to answer later and yet again I had to fix the mess he made. This was the reason he had been put on child support years prior. There was always a mishap when dealing with her dad. Baby girl needed guaranteed financial means. Although we never used her child support for her parties, her dad and I always paid for them together. We didn't agree on a lot of things but for baby girl we usually came together. I had to admit he usually supported her birthday parties no matter what. This year was different. Things really seemed to be over.

Her birthday party was a success and she knew he wasn't there. She surprised me, she asked to call him. She didn't even ask until the next day, she was learning not to ruin her good time because of the mistakes of others. She wanted to know why. I gave her the phone, he had to answer for himself. He wasn't happy because she called to question him, he thought I told her to call. She wanted to know, so I directed her to the person that would have the answers. Baby girl was intelligent, she knew there was a problem and she knew she had to ask him. This transition was hard for all of us, especially for a young mind to understand.

There's No Progress Without Opposition

"Always see the progress in your process."

I ALWAYS QUESTIONED MY CAREER path. I was a retail customer service manager and my biggest struggle was dealing with people. Everything God does is strategic, it was not by mistake I was placed in a position where I would be tested daily to conquer one of my biggest struggles. I had a problem biting my tongue. I struggled with listening to people complain all day about petty issues. How did I end up in customer service? God did it. I used to dread work every day. The customers had a problem with everything. My best solutions to their problems were not worthy of their time. My ex, boyfriend at the time, was taking me through hell, and it came with me to work. The customers didn't know I had all kinds of craziness going on at my house, neither was I aware of what was going on in their home. My life was a tornado every day and I was sinking under the pressure.

After my ex and I split, work didn't seem so bad. I didn't have a double portion of drama, so I could handle the issues at work better.

I also considered the attitudes of our customers could be attributed to issues at they had at home just as mine were. With that in mind, I approached situations with a new attitude. I had a mercy with them because I realized God had given me endless mercy in my situations. I learned to control my reactions to things customers said to me. I actually thought of my answers before I blurted them out. I took the time to consider all aspects of decisions before I made a final one. I wasn't so cut throat and mean to people.

In my walk with God, learning to love like him is a challenge. Sometimes we want to give people what they deserve and cut them down. When I consider all the times God could have cut me down, I reconsider my decision to retaliate against those that have done wrong against me. I've realized that the battle is best fought when we let God fight it for us. It's one of the most difficult concepts for us to carry out but it is imperative to let God be ruler and we be patient and let him do his perfect work.

One of my favorite stories in the bible is the story of Saul and David. Saul was appointed King by God and was given strict instructions by God to destroy the Amalekites and everything connected to them. Saul kills most of the Amalekites but keeps some of their best sheep and cattle to offer as a sacrifice to God. God is angry because Saul did not do as he said and rejects Saul as King.

God sends his Prophet Samuel out to appoint a new king to replace Saul. God tells Samuel the new King is at the house of Jesse. After going through all the other sons, Samuel asks Jesse if he had any more sons. Jesse informs Samuel that he does have one more son named David. David was the youngest son, and a shepherd boy. He was outside tending the sheep and was not considered for the position as King amongst the other sons of Jesse. What I loved most about this story was that David had a dirty job of tending sheep. He was on the bottom of the totem pole. He had been rejected by his family for the position as king because he appeared to be unqualified. What's amazing about this story is that while it is true David wasn't king material he was chosen by God. Jesse called David in from the fields. When Samuel saw David, God spoke to the prophet and told him that

David was the next King! Many times, in life we seem unqualified and those around us have counted us out. People will sit you on the sideline when God has set you up for a promotion. It's so refreshing to know that even when you've been rejected and left out in the fields that God will still raise you up.

As the story goes on, and Saul's reign as king is dwindling, he has set out to kill David. Saul has made it his mission to kill David because of his favor with God and people. In life, people will not like us because of the favor we have on our lives. They will make it their business to make your life miserable. Two times in the story of Saul and David, David had the opportunity to kill Saul. Even though David had every reason to take Saul's life he knew that Saul was still God's appointed king. David decided to let God deal with Saul and keep his hands clean. How many times have you heard "hold your peace and let the Lord fight your battles"? Saul repeatedly chased David and tried to kill him. Saul went into a cave to use the bathroom and David was hiding in the cave. David was so close to Saul that he was able to cut a piece of his robe. When Saul was out of the cave David called out to him to show him the robe he had cut. Saul was grateful that David hadn't killed him, but not enough to stop his pursuit to kill him. Some are not grateful of the grace you give them. Even when they act as if they are, they tend to still cut you down behind your back. Retaliation is still not necessary. No matter what people do to you, they too are God's children. Even when they are wrong, they also belong to God. I've struggled with my responses to those who hurt me. I've learned I can only be responsible for my actions and I have to remain right to get the blessings God has for me. So, I have made up in my mind to do as David has done and let him handle the "Saul's" in my life.

Another great point in David's story is when the Philistine's send him home form the battle. When he gets home, his family, livestock, and goods have all been captured. The Amalekites have burned down David's town of Ziklag. David asks God she her pursue those that have raided his town. God speaks to go after them. David runs into an Egyptian slave that leads him to the culprits and David attacks those that had taken he and his soldier's families and other belongings. The Bible says that "David brought back everything that had been stolen including their livestock. David also took the sheep and cattle that the Amalekites had with them." David did what God said. He didn't move unless God gave him the go ahead. David recovered everything that the enemy had taken from him and more because he was obedient to God's word when he told him to move. God's word is relevant today if we would apply it to our lives. David recovered all because he obeyed God. I plan on going into the enemy's camp and taking back everything that belongs to me as well. When God gives instructions, we should have an ear to listen and feet to move.

Eventually, in the story Saul is surrounded while in battle and kills himself by his own sword. David didn't have to lift a finger. David spent years running from Saul. Saul's son Johnathan was David's best friend. The hate Saul had for David separated the two friends. Even though they didn't see each other, they made a pact to always be loyal to each other's family. Sadly, Johnathan was killed in the war alongside his father Saul. Years later after Saul and Johnathan's death, David located Johnathan's son. David returned everything to Johnathan's son that his father and grandfather Saul had earned during his reign as king. He vowed to take care of him just as he had promised his father, Johnathan. Johnathan and David were the perfect example of a true friendship. No matter who disapproved of their friendship they were loyal. Even when death came between them their loyalty remained. When we experience struggles in our lives there are very few people that remain with us. We have to appreciate the loyal people just as David did and honor their dedication even when it wasn't convenient for them to stay.

After Samuel found David as a young shepherd in the field, he still faced many trials in his life. David fought for his life and nearly lost everything, but it never changed God's calling on his life. David went through a long process before he was officially appointed king. He knew he would be king ahead of time but the process between the time he got the word and the actual blessing was grueling. By the time David was king, he was already a skilled solider in battle. He had many notable battles under his belt. The conflict he faced running from Saul and the fighting the Amalekites prepared him to reign as a successful king. Just as David, we will face many trials before we see God's promise fulfilled in our lives. It does not mean God has forgotten us. The promise is still good, but the problems in between are what prepare us to appreciate the promise even more.

David's process taught him the lesson of loyalty and the compassion he displayed compassion he displayed during his process allowed him to care for the people of Israel the same way. David's life is a great example of how the promise of God does not exempt one from tests and trails. His life also shows how no matter how fierce the attack of the enemy, nothing can change God's promise he's made to you.

ATTITUDE OF GRATITUDE

"Gratefulness is our way of showing God we appreciate his mercy towards us, and it increases our faith that if he did it before, he surely can do it again."

I T'S NEVER GOOD TO envy what God is doing in someone else's life. Things always look perfect on the outside, but it is a fact that every person has a battle they are fighting. Tangible blessings create a façade of a perfect life. In reality, those that are blessed monetarily long for the things money can't buy. Luxury cars, massive estates, and big bank accounts seems like they should equal a happy life, but the halls of those mansions aren't filled with laughter or met by the embrace of loved ones. They are empty; beautiful, big, and empty. On the other hand, while when one goes home to a small two-bedroom apartment and baby girl meets you at the door, kisses and hugs are overflowing. Love lives there, in that small cramped space. Your motivation is housed in that small place. Would you trade that love for the empty mansion? We all have to learn to stay in our designated lanes and focus on what we have going on. I have learned to be grateful for what I have, lusting after material things only blinds us to the valuables, we already own. Intangible things hold more value than any push to start vehicle could ever give you. Love, peace, sanity, joy cannot be seen but I wouldn't trade any of these for all the money in the world. An attitude of gratitude is necessary.

I wanted to show baby girl to know how blessed she is. During Christmas time she donated money to Salvation Army's bell ringers. The bell ringer to expressed the significance of her putting the money in the bucket. Fortunately, she hasn't had to experience times where food is scarce. She doesn't know what it's like to not be able to choose what you would wear. Because she is an only child, she's not the best at sharing. Everything belongs to her. She had developed a selfish attitude. A major principle of the Christian faith is to love others as you love yourself. I wanted to make sure baby girl had a clear understanding that giving was better than keeping material things for yourself. I realized that outside of family and friends, giving was rare. I asked myself, "What have you given to someone you don't know with no strings attached?" "Have you carried out random acts of kindness just to brighten someone's day?" "What cause am I passionate about and what action have I taken to support it?" Families go without every day, life is hard for so many. I wanted to be an encourager, to uplift those who had fallen on hard times no matter the reason. I knew what it felt like to be low, to lose hope. I emptied out baby girl's clothes from previous years and gave them to a family that was having a hard time. I felt a feeling I hadn't felt before. The feeling of making a difference. God had blessed me with enough to where I could give some away. I wasn't rich, I had bills due, but I knew that while on my journey I had to do more that take, I had to give. I used to sell baby girl's clothes she couldn't wear to get extra money; this year was going to be different. Yes, they were quality items and yes, I needed the money, but you have to be a blessing. Every day I was making progress. Too often we want blessings and we never give. Demanding God to give us all the desires of our heart but we are not willing to do the very thing we are asking God to do. I had to further look at myself and evaluate my life. Was I giving on the same level I was expecting to receive? I was reinventing the person I had become. I was selfish, mean, high and mighty. God had shown me the error of my ways. I was learning to give selflessly. I wanted God to be pleased.

Who's in your circle?

T HE DELETION OF PEOPLE from your life has to happen at some point in all of our lives. The people around you help shape the drive and ambition you possess. Who's in your circle? Are all your friends just like you? We get so afraid to make decisions for ourselves, we give control to people who don't deserve it. We let them invade our space with their negative thoughts and lackluster characters, and they begin to rub off on us. Take charge of your circle, and delete the people who are not complimenting the person you want to be. Honesty is key. I want people who will tell me the truth no matter the circumstance. "Yes-men" are enablers. Some people thrive off people who will agree for the sake of validation. I need a group of friends that will call me out and tell me when I'm wrong. We've made the mistake of calling brutally honest friends haters or labeled them as toxic. These are the ones we need because if they are honest with pure motives, they are true friends,

In my relationship, I made the mistake of changing to fit what I thought he wanted me to be. I needed him to be happy with the things I did for him. I cooked, cleaned, and washed his clothes to prove I was wife material. I supported him to prove I would always be there. I gave him everything I had to prove to him I was the person I said I was. I didn't realize that I was trying so hard for his approval. Why? He wasn't doing much of anything to prove to me he was husband material. He faked it. I've learned not give husband privileges to a boyfriend. He had no reason to marry me, because he was already receiving the benefits without the commitment. He didn't have to commit to me, there was nothing else to work for. He had hit the jackpot, and I was the slot machine spitting out the golden coins. He put in just enough effort to keep my complaints at bay. True friends and loved ones accept you for who you are and appreciate your good deeds. They don't continually take with no intentions of reciprocation. It is best to get manipulative and greedy people away from you. I didn't expect the world from him. I would have taken the moon and the stars if that were all he had to give. I often said I just wanted all of him, but maybe the love he gave was all he had. Maybe my ex was doing what he knew how to do, what he saw modeled in his own home. I wasn't sure why he loved the way he did, but I knew it wasn't what I needed. I was looking for an equal partner that pushed just as hard as I did. He was sharing himself with everybody, and I was selfish I wanted it all for myself. I questioned if what I was looking for existed. It seemed that a lack of commitment was the new normal for relationships. I wasn't willing to compromise just for the sake of companionship, I knew I was looking for a rare breed, but I was tired of settling for good enough. I wanted the man God had created for me. I had to cut away the dead weight to make room for my promise.

Besides relationships, there are some friendships we allow in our lives that tend to be negative. They are vibe killers, and their energy will transfer to you. The glass is always half empty with these kinds of people. When you are in a great mood, excited about your day, a negative person can call and completely change your mood. They dump junk, treat you like a landfill. They give you all their garbage and filth and leave you with the nasty clean up. The power of positivity is amazing. When two people's energy are at same level or greater, they feed off each other. Empowerment is at its best when positive people agree. When you are sad, they can encourage you. A negative person will just make it worse, make your dark days darker. That's why it's great to have a positive person around to pull you out of the dumps and let you know everything is going to be fine. Where you are weak, you need a friend that's strong. God cuts away people we don't need in our lives. When this pruning happens, we must look to him for our strength. When my ex and I split, the validation I received from him was absent. Many times, I wasn't sure what I felt because I didn't have that affirmation. In this season of standing along, I found God's strength to be made perfect in my weakest moments. When you have inspirational people in your circle, they will remind you of God's strength. Motivated people want you to be just as motivated as them.

God gives us people to be the resources that we lack, and vice versa. Sometimes we feel like we missed out on certain relational perks by not having certain people in our lives. Many hurt because they didn't have a father, or a nurturing mother, but God makes those things work in our favor over time. The situations that used to be an excuse can be used as motivation to push us to work harder. If God thought, we needed the things we lost or didn't get at all to fulfill his purpose he wouldn't have left it out. He has given us what we need to make our dreams come true. The perspective that views our issues as a hindrance instead of an advantage is what's crippling our promotions in life. Having people around you to help shift your perspective is important to anyone that wants to go to the next level.

There are some people who are intimidated by your success. Even if you are not successful, the yearning to be better may make some uncomfortable. No one should ever make you feel bad for wanting to better yourself. That's why it's important to entertain those that have goals and the corresponding action to reach them. It's hard to intimidate those who run at an extraordinary pace towards destiny just as you do. Having goal –oriented people in your circle means that everyone is pressing toward the mark and there is not time for jealousy. If one friend reaches the finish line before the other, they are willing to provide guidance to help those after him.

There are also those that want to ride your coat tail. There is nothing wrong with partnering with those who are willing to work just as hard as you. They are there through your wins and losses. Watch the ones show up when its show time. They didn't put in any work behind the scenes but want all the glory. I've always been the friend that will answer the phone in the wee hours of the morning and the late-night hours, whenever I was there. Those that miss calls and don't return them, but don't hesitate to pick up the phone when they need you are the friends that need to be cut out of our lives. God blesses those who help with no motive, no strings attached, and want nothing in return. Many help to acquire bragging right, but genuine friends keep no record of what they have done for you.

I've had some friends that are not in my life as much as they used to be. It's not because I don't love them, it's simply because we out grew each other. Our lives took us in different directions, and that's ok. I can still call on them if I need them, even if I hadn't talked to them in months. I accepted the fact that God taught me to stand alone. They weren't a negative influence in my life, because I had learned the importance of surrounding yourself with go-getters. But because we all had a hunger inside of us. We went after what we wanted and understood that we couldn't take each other along for the ride. Real friends understand that only distance can separate you, the love you have for each other never changes.

Set the Standard

"As life progresses, we have some standards that we have to set for ourselves and those around us. This is the foundation of all relationships we encounter. They are the key characteristics we look for in the people we allow in our lives. They cannot be compromised."

G OD IS A FORGIVING God and gives us all chances we don't deserve, but I also know my name is not Jesus. He gave the greatest sacrifice for us and he has redeemed us all if we choose to take advantage. He also gives us discernment, the ability to choose and decide what's best for ourselves. Being spiritually connected to God allows us to use our discernment to choose who influences us, and who has access to us. I have always been a person to give chances, and I still am.

Life has taught me to take a closer look at those around me. I have put so much effort in to changing my life I realize I can't let everyone in. I have to protect my energy, my influences, my surroundings have to be conducive to my destiny. I am more selective with who I associate with. I've found that trust, loyalty and consistency are a few areas where my standard has been set and will not waiver. Setting the standard has nothing to do with physical requirements of a mate or friend. I am speaking to the character of those we entertain. The outward appearance is at the bottom of the list after you have dealt with someone who has character flaws.

Trusting someone is one of the most difficult things to do when it's been violated so many times. I've decided to trust, and if in any way I see that my trust is being violated then I cannot lower my standard and give numerous chances. I have to understand that this person is not worthy of my trust and has to be deleted from my life. Separating yourself from someone that you have become attached is hard, but if we want to go to higher heights all dead weight must be disposed of, liars included.

Loyalty is another standard that has become one of my deal maker or breakers. In my relationship, I was loyal. I was dedicated to my little family no matter what came about. I made decisions based on how they would affect baby girl and her dad before mine. Being loyal is honorable, but don't be anyone's fool. Some people change with the wind. One day they are your biggest supporter, but somewhere along the way they change into your biggest hater. They change without notice. Minor unfavorable circumstances sway loyal people. It uncovers their lack of dedication. When you deal with loyal people, they vow to stand with you even when times are hard and are still standing behind you when the situation improves.

Consistency is also important. It ties in with loyalty. People can be either consistently dependable or a consistent let down. Which are you to those around you? Do you always come through in the clutch, or are you the one who can never make it? We all set standards and have things we accept and won't accept, but make sure you are the person you want to have. I don't just set standards and then break them in my own life. I have vowed to be the person I want to see in others. I want trust because I'm trustworthy. I demand loyalty because I am loyal. Consistency is a must because I make it a point to be consistent. When you get me, you get all these things among others. Many people think you are full of yourself when you know your worth. I have found that knowing your worth and setting standards is protection. It's guarding your heart and ridding yourself of those who threaten your peace. When I look back over past situations, I see how I didn't have any standards. I let people come in and out and treat me any kind of way. Now I know that my savior thought I was worth dying for. So, because he thought I was worth so much, I know that I cannot give people the power to mistreat me. When you know your worth, you demand nothing less than what you deserve. If you bring loyalty, consistency, and trustworthiness, then why would it be fair to let a liar come in and tear your world apart? It's not ok for inconsistent people to put you on hold until they need you, you deserve someone to love you the same way you love them. Yes, people do love differently, but if our love is not compatible then it's best to move on and find a love that matches your own.

When I began this journey, it was hard for me to understand people who don't demand the best for themselves. I had to realize that the same journey to understanding I had to take, they also have to travel. Once we all realize that everyone is on a journey to their destiny, we can forgive what they have done to us a little easier. It's not a crime to get rid of toxic people, but realize they too, are on a journey. You may be farther along than they are, but it's dangerous to your path if you try to take those along with you that don't belong. Don't allow their journey to stop yours. There is nothing wrong with letting them go on their destined path without you. I find myself praying all the time for God to guide me in the right direction. I don't want anything or anyone that is not for me. I want the things God has prepared for me and nothing else. Your standards are synonymous to the foundation of a home. The integrity of the entire structure rests on how strong the foundation is. Make sure your foundation is sound, unmovable even when storms come. There are no room for cracks, sinking, or compromise.

Don't Go Back

"Don't live life with regrets. God will send us reminders to confirm that the decisions we made were for the best."

I T WAS A TYPICAL morning, I was combing baby girl's hair and preparing to take her to school. He called at his typical time to tell her to have a good day. After their conversation was over and they said their goodbyes he asked to speak to me. I'm not sure what he wanted, maybe it was to ask about what she wanted for Christmas. "Hey, what you doing?" "Nothing." "Well, what do you want for Christmas?" I giggled because I knew that this was about to be pure and utter foolishness. "I don't want anything for Christmas." "Oh ok, do you still like candles?" "Yea, but I'm good, the things I have ever wanted money couldn't buy." "Oh yea? And what's that?" I have known this guy for nine years, and I knew then he still didn't know me. Year after year, for my birthday and Christmas he always asks me what I wanted. I was never a material girl because I was able to provide those things for myself. I worked hard and depended on God for the rest, so I was good when it came to material things. "All I've ever wanted was love, peace, and happiness. And I have that now so I'm good." That statement threw him for a loop. I knew his mind would wonder and settle on what it sounded like on the surface. What he didn't know was that I had found all those things within myself. I took him out of the equation and learned to depend on God to guide me to his purpose for my life. He led me to the person he wanted me to do and put my mind to do his work only. "Oh, so you are in a relationship?" "No, I'm not." "Well what you talking about?" I didn't want to get deep because I wasn't sure if his mind could think on that level. I explained how I depended on him for happiness and when I had to stand alone, I learned how to be happiness with me. I took control back and was running full speed ahead. I realized that in all his questioning he never inquired about baby girl. It had been seven months and he had visited with her twice. One of those times I made it happen. Anger began to grow, and I couldn't hold my thoughts in any longer. "You have managed to ask me a lot of questions pertaining to my business. What baffles me the most is you have yet to make arrangements with me to see your child. She went from seeing you at least twice every two weeks to twice in months. Why is that not a concern of yours? She's trying to adjust to her new life, and you haven't tried to make this a comfortable transition for her. You have left me with all the tough questions and the cleanup, and you are just living your life." "Renèe I have been working for six to seven weeks at a time." "Ok and that's fine but when you get home, why haven't you tried to spend time with her? She needs to know that you still love her. Before you get in my business you make sure you ask about baby girl. Make sure she is good. I'm still waiting on the school shoes you got her. I'm still waiting on the money you owe me from her birthday party. You turned her life upside down and you aren't even concerned with her emotions. She's been abandoned by you, why doesn't that bother you? The fact that I may be with another man worries you more that your child's emotions. Put your priorities in order ok. I'm not your business, she is!" There was silence. He knew he didn't have a rebuttal to the valid point I made. I hadn't cursed in months because I hadn't been agitated to that degree since we had broken up. I was reminded of what I felt months ago. The anger and aggravation I had risen in me was reminiscent of that in our relationship. I didn't like that feeling, I hated how he made me feel. It was confirmation that he hadn't changed and that I would never go back. I thought about my baby and how I had to change her life. I had to get away from the negativity of her daddy and in turn it had changed her also. I was doing my best to make it right, and he was doing his best to take me back to the dark place. I wasn't willing to go. This conversation had taken me to the doorway of the dark place, and I was determined not to walk in. I had to reel myself back to me, I had to hang up. I had to stop this conversation. I left him with this thought, "Our baby's world had been shaken up, and you need to help me get it back to something like what it once was. I am not your concern, make time for her ok. That's all you need to worry about." I was crying because nothing upset me more than the emotional stress baby girl may have experienced in this ordeal. She was everything to me and I wanted to ensure she was in a good place. Even if it meant standing at the doorway of the dark place. I had pleaded her case and I hoped he taken heed. It was hard to say if he understood or not. He kept trying to call after I ended our conversation. There was nothing else to say, all he needed to do was step up.

While in this conversation I realized something, he was delusional. He didn't take responsibility for any of his mess. He still didn't admit he helped ruin our little family. He said nothing was ever good enough for me. He said no matter what he did I always complained. I told him, "During the course of our relationship I only wanted your time, and that was the very thing you weren't willing to give." He thought gifts would make me happy, he thought dinner dates would satisfy me. I wanted something on a deep level. I wanted my soul to be satisfied. I wanted his love, companionship, but most of all I wanted his time. He wasn't willing to give me that and I had accepted that. I was fine with it. I had made peace with my past, and I wasn't going back to give him a chance to give me what he just confirmed he didn't have. It was a learning experience, it taught me to be happy with me and find everything else I needed in the almighty. God was there to pat me on the back after this conversation. Everything had come full circle. I realized that man couldn't give me anything I needed. Everything I needed came directly from God. He knows what I needed. So, I made up in my mind to wait on who he was going to send to love me and be my life partner. The alone time God was giving me wasn't to punish me, it was to prepare me to accept the love he set aside for me. This time was to tie up loose ends, get rid of any bitterness left. The love that was on its way was getting the best version of me, the me that had been tried and tested and proven to be true.

The Table He Prepared

"God will move in a tremendous way on your behalf just to show his power. Those who were against you will realize that only God could have made it happen."

P SALM 23:5 SAYS THAT "Thou preparest a table before me in the presence of mine enemies; thou anointest my head with oil; my cup runneth over." I have heard that scripture so many times, yet never really understood what it meant until I had a little trouble in my life. The scripture is written by David whose job in the bible was to be a shepherd of his father's sheep. He used this metaphor to describe the way God takes care of us, the same way David did the sheep. Sheep are not the smartest animals and are vulnerable to wolves. The shepherd's job is to make sure the sheep are safe and unharmed while grazing. Sheep have short legs and can't run fast, so the job of the shepherd was crucial to their survival.

I was preparing my lunch for work one day, and I began to question why God kept me connected to baby girl's father. I loved my baby and wouldn't trade her for the world, but the fact that he wasn't permanent in my life but was still present confused me. That's when this scripture came to me and explained it all. How can he prepare a table before me in the presence of my enemies, if they aren't present in my life to see it? I don't see him as an evil force, but his actions carried out in my life were those of an enemy. He carried himself as a person that didn't want to see me win. God brought me to the realization that he would seat me at the table and allow me to feast and show how the weapons formed didn't prosper. This is not to be taken as a literal table and a big Thanksgiving feast, but it is the table of life. Growing in adversity, becoming better, rising above the hurt, and being successful despite of the things that should have taken you out. That's the feast.

When I looked back over my circumstances, I realized that no matter how bad things got, the shepherd was there the whole time. He was there watching my situations and making sure, that when it was all said and done, I wasn't harmed. I've learned that as long and God is with me, there is nothing that I want or should long for because he will supply all my needs, hence the line "I shall not want." The still waters that the scripture speaks of can attest to the peace of mind I have found in him. There is also a line that says, "he restoreth my soul." For the longest time, I felt like my joy had been stolen from me. I was lost and confused after everything fell apart. Now I live every day in a different light, he has truly restored my soul. He has given me joy and peace back. I cherish them so much more now, because I know what it's like to not have them. My journey has given me a spirit of gratefulness that is stronger than ever.

We all encounter valleys in our life, but it is such a comfort to know that "Though I walk through the valley of the shadow of death, I will fear no evil, for thou art with me." So many times, I felt alone throughout the miscarriages and various hurts, but truth be told, I never was. Those were the times he was there the most. The 23rd Psalm is a summary of life basically. David wrote this Psalm so well that it has lasted centuries and resonated with people from many walks of life. It gives comfort in hard times and assures of that because our shepherd is concerned about his flock, there will be redemption if we just hold on.

A moment of redemption came for me when it was time to get baby girl's Christmas gifts from her dad. He called and asked me to meet him. I asked, "I have to come meet you?" He replied "Yes, I'm not coming all the way down there, and I'm not coming to your grandmother's house." Even though I was tired, had worked the Saturday night before, and had gotten up early the next morning to prepare for church, I was still willing to take her to see her father. After church, we changed and took to the road. She was excited. Some don't understand a true mother's sacrifice. We traveled thirty minutes met in a restaurant parking lot and he put her gifts in my car. She opened a few. Baby girl says, "Daddy, can we go and get something to eat? Me, you and my mama?" She spotted a Chinese food buffet, pointed, and he obliged. She wanted things to be like old times. I agreed. There weren't any hard feelings, I didn't treat him coldly. We even shared a few laughs, I wasn't bitter. Baby girl was talking about the church service we enjoyed earlier that day. "Daddy, my mama sang a song at church today." He said, "Oh really?" He shifted his focus to me, "So you're leading songs at church now? You've been cutting up, huh?" I felt proud because I had faced one of my greatest fears, I had sung God's glory in front of everyone, and I think baby girl was proud of me, too. This was a testament to how I had changed, I had come out of my shell. My trials had given me courage. He knew I had found my voice, my courage, the real me.

I felt in my spirit that this was my season. It was my time to demonstrate just how amazing God's grace was. I reflected on our day during the drive home. I had faced my fears, had sat in the presence of my ex without have great anger rise inside of me. One thing that really stood out from church earlier, the moment Bishop prayed for me. He laid hands on me, prayed, and I was getting ready to walk away. He pulled me back, I was confused. His eyes met mine, and in his most sincere voice he said, "God told me to tell you he was going to fix it. Do you believe God?" I replied "Yes." I was emotional, because for years I had gone through many prayer lines with no prophecy. No word from God, he was silent most of the time. This time God had a word for me, confirmation that everything was going to be ok. He sent word through his messenger that my solution was coming, that he would fix everything that was broken. That was all I needed to hear. God knows the desires of my heart and, because I actively sought after his will for my life, he would reward me. God said he was going to fix it.

YOU HAVE WHAT YOU NEED

"The things we have lost along the way are not necessary to accomplish the plan God has for us. Had it been necessary it would have never left."

ONE OF THE MOST valuable lessons I have learned on this journey is that whatever you need to win, God has already given it to you. We spend our lives looking for that something or someone to complete us. Everything we need to fulfill God's plan for our lives is inside of us. If it's not within us, he will place people in your path that will serve as resources for whatever you lack. Many of us go through life thinking we aren't enough. Education, money, upbringing are all things people think will make a difference in reaching their destiny. If God thought, we needed those things then he would provide a means for us to get them. One of the greatest things in life is to overcome its adversities. That's the part that makes success and living a happy life that much better because of the struggle, the thing that was conquered. It makes each of us special. Our problems and deficiencies make us individuals, if we all needed money and education to make it to the top them what would make the rise special? Some of the most successful people came from a struggle.

I've realized that doubt will keep you from your destiny. Circumstances seem unfavorable and situations discourage us. What I've learned is that when things seem impossible, God takes it as an opportunity to make miracles happen. Many of the difficult places we find ourselves in are a set-up, to position us.

I started this journey, fired up and ready to write my book. I was encouraged and hit the ground running. I didn't realize that it would be hard work, and I didn't know it would be expensive. I wasn't born with a silver spoon nor was a working a six-figure job. The money I made was to take care of my child and me. My responsibility as a mother was to make sure we had reliable transportation and roof over our head, clothing and food. I graduated college, I worked as a manager, but there was no room to finance a book. I was torn between doing what God instructed me to do and taking care of my obligations. I didn't see how. I didn't understand why he would give me a vision that I couldn't make come to life. All the faith I had, all the praying I had done I still doubted God. At some point in our lives we all question God. I knew that God always made a way, but my situation didn't seem to be changing and it had been months since he spoke to me. I thought about Bishop telling me God said he was going to fix it. So, I made my mind up to be patient, but I wasn't. I became anxious.

I was working one day and one of my favorite customers came into the store. We hugged and began to chat. He always got the latest on the happenings in my life. After laughing it up for a while I realized something. My good friend I had grown close to, worked at the parish library. He attended book conferences galore and had may have the connections I needed to get me started as a writer. I asked him, "Hey do you know any book publishers?" He replied, "Yea, I know a few. Who's writing a book?' I explained to him I was in the process of telling the story of my journey and I was going to need his help. He agreed to help me with whatever I needed and said if I finished in time, he could take my book with him to the annual book conference he attended every June. God seemed to be working in my favor. I had to let the words flow through my fingertips and onto my computer screen. I had to finish what I started.

At this point I had written much of the book and it was almost time for the editing process. One of my co-workers was an English major and I had given him the rough draft to get it ready to send to do a final edit. I began to get quotes and it seemed to be a pretty steep price to get a book edited. I was worried. It was weighing heavy on my mind on the commute to work one day. I said a prayer and told God "Lord I don't have enough. I need your help." I had asked God to help me and send me the connections to finish what he started. When I got to work, I realized I had to work in the copy center. The busiest area of the store, and I was not thrilled. I was multitasking times ten and I was tired. A lady walked in with a business card she wanted recreated. I realized that the business card was for a book editor. I was stunned. After looking at the lady again I realized she was a local author that had written and published three books of her own. I asked her, "You've written books before, right?" She replied, "Yes, actually I have written and published three books." In my mind I was amazed at how fast God had worked. I continued to talk to the author. I picked her brain on a few things and she invited me to a book conference that would be held later that year. Not only had I found a potential editor, I had gotten some answers from the horse's mouth. I was so grateful to God for sending these connections my way. Whenever I begin to doubt him, he always sent confirmation that I was on the right path. I wrestled with the path I was taking many times. I believed he was leading me, and it wasn't any doing of my own. I knew that if I followed his divine destiny that there was no room for failure.

For years, I had planned on leaving my job. The customers were rough, and I left with a headache daily. Little by little God's plan was being unveiled. I understood why I never got any job I applied for. Even when the interviews went perfect, I never received a call back. I had to be still. The rejection I had gotten from the other jobs weren't because I wasn't qualified. I didn't get them because my destiny was inside the four walls of my current job. The place that I would have never been if I would have gone to hair school. I was in this town because I had gone to the university located there, I was at this job because a girl in my university English class worked there. She helped me get the job. I graduated from the university, got promoted months later. The promotion wasn't in the same store. It required me to move back home. I went to the new store, only to transfer back to where I started. I moved from my parent's house, into the house that I had inherited from my grandfather. My old store was closer. Destiny had taken me back where I started. Back to the town my university was in, back to the place that was second on my list, but first on God's list. I had been with the company nine years. Every day I looked for a new job, I was miserable. The money was good, but I wasn't prepared for the emotional stress it would give me. Every day I heard complaining, irrational people that wanted impossible results from me. They always said, "Let me speak to the manager!" I would come, short in stature, young and female. "Are you the manager?" I begged God to recuse me from these mean people. I was wasting my time.

He was teaching me how to handle conflict. How to stand when everything seemed to fall apart. At the time I was failing miserably because I had conflict at home, work, and within myself. Life was rough for me during those years. Sometimes I went home and cried. I didn't know God had placed me where I would discover connections to destiny. Everything I needed was at my job and I was fighting it. God has a way of positioning you, even when it feels like punishment. His ways are so amazing. I reflect on how I got to where I am, and it amazes me how he orchestrated the events of my life so that I would be in the right place and the right time. I often ask myself, "Where would I be without the Lord?"

One thing remained, I was still single. I thought I had done an excellent job improving my own life. What happens when you give your life to God and nothing seems to get better? The area of my life where I had the greatest. Why was I still alone? I had to realize, once again, that my timing and God's timing may differ.

God wanted alone time with me. Every day we talked, every day I learned something new about him. I realized that preparation for a blessing isn't a quick process. Together, God and I, had to finish what we started. My soul still needed love, I still had healing to do and I had to be alone to get it done. God had touched me in places that no man could ever. He had given me unconditional love that no partner could exceed. He had fulfilled promises that others broke. He wanted the best for me, and I had to stop questioning him and trust him. I had to realize its ok to not understand. It's ok to question God, because he takes that opportunity to show his great power. I wasn't ready yet, he still had some kinks to work out in me and I had to be calm and let him work. I talked to my friends, I thought maybe they could shed some light. We were deep in conversation and I said, "I'm just tired of waiting!" I heard myself, my eyes bucked, I said "I got it! He's teaching me patience." I thought I had gotten that lesson years ago when I waited for love, but obviously I needed a refresher course. Since I hadn't completed my book, I figured God would at least work a miracle in my love life. Everything seemed to be at a standstill. But when I heard myself say I was tired of waiting, I knew I had to shut my mouth and see what God was trying to show me. I realized that this quiet time was to improve myself. I wanted to hear I love yous and wanted hugs, but I was still impatient. I was still rushing. Life had taught me to look deeper into situations and not skim the surface. I had cracked the code, but I was still struggling. Renée was in the midst of a patience lesson and so far, had failed. I needed to be self-sufficient and focus on the gifts God had given me and sharpen them.

God had blessed me with more than one talent. It was time to pursue them all. The New Year seemed like it was going to be a busy one. Doubt began to make its way back because it seemed as if I was biting off more than I could chew. Time and money were the odds that were stacked against me, I asked "Lord who do you think I am? Superwoman?" A book, church activities, a full-time job and not to mention my mommy duties. I knew he wasn't going to give me more than I could bear. He was positioning me to prosper and I had to accept the challenge.

The paths our lives take are predestined. In the dark places and happy places, he's teaching and positioning us. I am grateful for all the jobs I didn't get, as well as the one I have. The times I cried and the times I smiled. The doors he opened and the ones he shut. The people he brought into my life as well as the ones he let leave. The rejection, conflict, hurt all conditioned me. I realize that the gifts that God has given us are ours. It's our duty to perfect those gifts and use them to his purpose. The enemy can't take our gifts from you, everything we need to win in within us. It takes will power and some tough circumstances to bring them to the forefront but when it's all over we realize that whatever we lacked wasn't necessary to our being. God doesn't take away what we need, he supplies our needs.

The circumstances can make you feel unqualified, but God qualifies the unqualified. He has placed many in positions that on paper, may seem they don't deserve. His favor trumps any degree or experience. The resources God provides will have your enemies at your foot wondering how you made it. That's how amazing he is. Many are searching for success in all the wrong places. I am a firm believer that when you seek him, he will reveal his purpose. If you are driven enough to chase after when he has put inside of you, success in inevitable

The climb to the top is what perfects our character. It shows the faith that we possess. Many pray and wait for a miracle, there is work involved. You have to have the intention to be blessed. There will be sleepless nights. There will be tears. There will be battles. The enemy will rise up against you. As long as you stay confident in the purpose he has for your life, your destiny will not change. Following Jesus is not easy, if anything the walk becomes more difficult. Many believe that bad things don't happen if you believe in God. There is no great triumph without great trials. When you have a God you can look to, that went through his own great trials you find strength to bear your own. His journey was not easy, and neither will yours. We all have our crosses to bear. The journey he has set for all of us gives us the strength we need once we reach the destination. I thought my life was out of control and just a mess, but some of the best results come from messy situations. Chaos in your life means God is up to something.

I've learned that there is a blessing in your brokenness. Strength in your stress, and miracles in your mess. Sometimes in life we try to rush to our destiny. Rush to see what the blessing are. My journey has been a long one, and it's not over. My destiny is the reward, but the most important things are what I've learned along the way. The lessons and trials along the way are preparing me for that place of purpose. Don't rush the journey because you will miss the things along the way.

I'm so excited to see what else God has for me but I will be patient. I know there are more lessons I will have to learn, I don't know it all. At the time it hurt, at the time it seemed important, now I know your current circumstance is only a temporary state. God has so much more promised for us if we would just consult with him and then move on his word.

When I didn't hear from God, I became frustrated. I wanted to make something happen, I wanted to force the outcome. I've learned to exercise my power of choice and to be happy with what is right and pray to God to reveal to me how to fix what's wrong. His fix is not the easiest most of the time but it's necessary. You have to be ready to do what he instructs. Even when we make mistakes God can turn those mistakes around for our good. Most of the hasty decisions we make arise from situations we try to fix on or own. It's not our battle to fight. Prayer has given me and dialogue with God that soothes all my uneasiness. It proves to me that if I just step aside and let him have his way it will turn out just fine. I've seen him do it in my life, that's how I know. Let him have his way, he will make it alright. Even after accepting that there would be battles, I always seemed to be caught off guard when the next one came. My ex said he missed me, and I didn't feel the same way. There used to be a time when those three words would fix everything, but it wasn't in the cards for him anymore. He hadn't got the memo that his time was up. A week had passed, and his girlfriend messaged me after seeing texts after our phone conversation. She wanted to know what he said to me. He made her think he hated me, she said all he did was call me disrespectful names and I supposedly kept baby girl away from him. I can't lie, it hurt me. I had worked so hard to improve the person I was, to hear someone was still dragging my name did something to me. "RENÈE, YOU ARE LYING! I NEVER CALLED YOU, I DON'T MISS YOU!" I hadn't had these harsh words spoken to me in so long, that I was shaken up. It reminded me of why our relationship had crashed and burned. I was fully convinced he was a demon. He outright lied and then cursed me out because he got caught. I told him to never call my phone again. God had given me the grace to handle his antics in our relationship, but I had lost that grace and I wasn't going to continue the abuse. I purchased baby girl her own cell phone and that's how she would talk to him. I was being harassed in a sense and it was becoming unbearable. I didn't want him, and I didn't want any more confusion. Oddly enough it prompted me to pray for him daily because it disturbed me. He needed God's help, he was the only one that could change the situation.

THE PERFECT STORM

"Chaos is God's opportunity to give us his peace. Our storms seem unbearable, but in reality, he knows how much pressure we need to push us into our destiny. God is the master at creating the most perfect storms."

WHEN IT WAS ALL said and done, God knew when to make the winds blow. He knew exactly when to make the flood waters rise. When to send the tornadoes of life to rip away my comfort zone. He sent the rain that blinded my sight and commanded hail fall and knock me down. The heat from the lies told drained my positive energy and the blizzards barricaded me in misery. He released the right amount of nature's fury to force me to seek shelter in him. The whole time I saw chaos, I realize he had it under control. Debris everywhere, I was standing its midst. My life was in shambles as I looked around accounting the damage, counting up the cost. The friendships lost, the laughs that were replaced by tears, the ache in my chest and somehow, I was still standing. Broken, hurt and maybe limping but still standing. The storm has passed, but where's the relief team? Who's going to help rebuild. I felt like I needed to call in a contractor with the necessary tools, so he could restore what was lost. This time I vowed to do it bigger, to come back stronger that I had ever been. Now I know to be more cautious and to seek shelter when the storm comes. Heed the warnings, see the signs, and don't ignore the blaring sirens. Every day the rebuilding process is progressing, soon the storm will be a memory. It has made me appreciate the sunshine. And even though it was a great shake up and earthquake of historical proportions, things were looking up. I went through a terrifying time, I thought my life was over. I made it, the sun was shining again. I realize the storm may had given way to brighter days. The storm's sting wasn't as great as it first seemed. They tear down to rebuild. Resurrect that which has fallen. Temporary displacement turned into permanent residency, new dwellings, my humble abode, living with the King by my side. Everything is new after the storm. I had withstood the winds, weathered the rain, the reward was surely to follow. God created the perfect storm and blow it blew me in the right direction.

What is God setting you up for? Are you embracing your destiny steps to get closer to your purpose or are you fighting the lessons? What amazed me most about my life thus far was how much I felt unworthy of the opportunities God had given me. I felt deep in my spirit that God had a greater life planned for me. I was on the verge of his blessings and I wasn't sure lil ole me was worth of the goodness of God knowing all the mistakes I had made. Despite of my life thus far he called me anyway. I'm up for the challenge. I realized God had my life was under control the entire time. I had endured the perfect storm, and it was time for the sun to shine again.

About the Author

The Perfect Storm is the real life story of a young girl from McComb, Mississippi and her first serious relationship. At 21, she meets her prince charming, and through a series of unfortunate events is left heartbroken and empty. Now 33, Reneè is using her journey to healing as a source of inspiration for other women. The Perfect Storm chronicles how she went from the lowest point in her life to the realization the entire time God was in control.

Printed in the United States
By Bookmasters